We dedicate this book to
Edy & Abner Ramos.
with love!

Aurea Nadasi

11-30-05

The ESCAPE

Aurea Nadasi

Cover Design and Illustrations
Nicole Campasano

Author: Aurea Nadasi
Translated by: Esther Nadasi Pruscino
Co-Edited by: Suzana Nadasi Pascual
Cover and Illlustrations by: Nicole Campasano – www.bnbdesignstudio.com

Note for Librarians: a cataloguing record for this book that includes Dewey Decimal Classification and US Library of Congress numbers is available from the Library and Archives of Canada. The complete cataloguing record can be obtained from their online database at: www.collectionscanada.ca/amicus/index-e.html
ISBN 1-4120-3002-1
Printed in Victoria, BC, Canada

Printed on paper with minimum 30% recycled fibre.
Trafford's print shop runs on "green energy" from solar, wind and other environmentally-friendly power sources.

TRAFFORD

Offices in Canada, USA, Ireland and UK
This book was published *on-demand* in cooperation with Trafford Publishing. On-demand publishing is a unique process and service of making a book available for retail sale to the public taking advantage of on-demand manufacturing and Internet marketing. On-demand publishing includes promotions, retail sales, manufacturing, order fulfilment, accounting and collecting royalties on behalf of the author.

Book sales for North America and international:
Trafford Publishing, 6E–2333 Government St.,
Victoria, BC v8t 4p4 CANADA
phone 250 383 6864 (toll-free 1 888 232 4444)
fax 250 383 6804; email to orders@trafford.com
Book sales in Europe:
Trafford Publishing (uk) Limited, 9 Park End Street, 2nd Floor
Oxford, UK oxi 1hh UNITED KINGDOM
phone 44 (0)1865 722 113 (local rate 0845 230 9601)
facsimile 44 (0)1865 722 868; info.uk@trafford.com
Order online at:
trafford.com/04-0829

10 9 8 7 6 5 4 3

I dedicate this book to my husband, Gustavo, who is the main character of this book and whose courage has always motivated me to go forward on the roads of life, even through obstacles that might appear impossible to break through. To this day, his brilliant personality doesn't cease to amaze me.

I also dedicate this book to my three children, Esther, Suzana and Gustavo Jr., who without doubt, are the three most beautiful flowers decorating the garden of my life.

ACKNOWLEDGEMENTS

Many thanks to my daughter, Esther, who faithfully occupied herself for so many days to translate this book from Portuguese to English, doing so in such a precise manner.

I thank my daughter, Suzana, for dedicating her time in co-editing this book, so kindly assisting me during the completion stages of this book.

Thanks to my son, Gustavo Jr., for helping me focus on my work and for thoughtfully supporting me in many different ways.

I also would like to thank my daughter-in-law, Michelle, as well as my sons-in-law, Angelo and Robert, for giving me so much support to complete this project.

Special thanks to my good friend Marilyn Harding who kindheartedly assisted me in reading and revising this book in its initial stage.

Thanks to my dear friends Delmer and Mary Frances Olds for referring me to this publisher.

And last but not least, I thank God, Who inspired me to finish this project. May this book be to His glory.

Many thanks to my dear friend, Nicole Campasano, the artist who has dedicated so much of her time designing the cover as well as the illustrations in this book. Nicole, you have made this book so much more complete by enriching it with your wonderful talent.

AUTHOR'S NOTES

I am deeply grateful to God, for being right beside me, guiding my steps as I wrote this book and finally published it.

When I met my husband Gustavo in the 1960's, he told me about his incredible past and journey in search of freedom. Since then, my heart has been filled with an intense desire to write the story of his life and to eventually publish it. My dream was that all who would have the opportunity to read this book would learn the atrocities done against innocent people and at the same time learn about God's love and mercy which was revealed in my husband's life. This mercy took him from the imprisonment of Communism and brought him to liberty, which he always dreamed of.

Even if I thanked God constantly throughout my life, there wouldn't be sufficient time to thank Him for giving me the privilege of having Gustavo as my husband, father of our children and grandfather of our grandchildren. I feel very blessed!

During the months (and so many months!) while I

worked on this project, I was always praising the Lord for I could feel His presence, constantly inspiring me as I was writing this book. Even before I started writing, I prayed and dedicated my work to the Lord.

And now, I hope you follow this incredible journey with your mind and spirit, a journey of a young man in search of freedom. I promise that after reading this book you will feel blessed for having an opportunity to participate in this journey of a life which had and still has the power of God's touch!

God bless you all and may you all feel in your own lives the power of God.

In His love,

Aurea Nadasi
Author

This book is a narrative of a true story. The name of the main character, Gustavo Nadasi, remains unchanged. However, the names of other characters have been changed for ethical and privacy reasons.

1

Budapest, Hungary - 1951

The night was delightful, the air was filled with a remarkable aroma from the flowers that beautified Margaret Island. The atmosphere induced one to retreat or, just simply, absorb the magic of nature. However, it was a special night. Gustavo left with his family, apparently for a simple walk to a hotel nearby. His parents offered ice cream to him and his brother, Jozsef, so they sat outside and waited for the treat. The live band initiated the first accords of a very well known song, and while listening to the music, Gustavo's heart started pounding as he thought about how he would tell his mother, so delighted sitting right beside him, everything that needed to be revealed.

"Here folks, take your ice creams! Strawberry for the guys, chocolate and vanilla for you", the waiter's voice interrupted the thoughts of young Gus.

"Thank you. Everything is fine!" replied Mr. Istvan Nadasi, Gustavo's father. An absolute silence came after, while the whole family enjoyed the ice cream. The sound of the orchestra enhanced the ambiance and induced them to dance. Jozsef soon noticed a beautiful young lady who was sitting at the table right next to them. For Jozsef, a young man of good appearance, handsome, twenty-four years of age, it was not difficult to note those captivating feminine eyes in search of his. A few minutes later, the ice cream was ignored. Soon, with impetus, Jozsef was beside the young lady requesting the honor of a dance.

The watchful eyes of Gustavo followed his brother and the young lady as they approached the dance floor and started to dance. This was the opportunity he had been waiting for to talk with his mother without his brother around.

"Mother! Let's dance!" Gus' lips were trembling in trying to smile at his mother while taking her to the dance floor.

The music was light and Eva rested her arms on her son's shoulders, proud and honored for the princely elegance by which he was leading the dance.

"I didn't know you could dance so well! I think today..."

"Mother!" Gus interrupted her cordially. "I have something to tell you... and my brother can't know anything about it." He placed his lips by his mother's ears. He was almost breathless, his voice trembled, but he was certain that this was the right moment to tell her.

"You scare me!" Eva replied. "What is it that you brother can't hear?"

"Mother, pretend everything is OK and just listen to me, please!"

Eva's smile and excited expression were gone, but she tried to do exactly what her son asked her to do.

"Are you kidding me? I bet you failed in one of the classes in school. Is that what you are trying to tell me?"

"Please, mother, I don't have too much time. It has got to be now since Jozsef is distracted with that young lady. If he finds out, he will impute me to the authorities..."

A dark shadow dropped onto Eva. She was a woman of strong personality, used to having things done her way, and all of a sudden, she felt powerless before a situation where she could not prevail upon.

"I can not stay in Budapest. I must escape!...Otherwise the authorities will send me to Siberia to do forced labor."

Astonished, Eva placed her lips by her son's ears and uttered, "I can not believe in what you're telling me. This is only a joke, isn't it?"

"Mother! Please, listen! I am telling you that I have to leave the country and I only have a few days to prepare everything..."

"But why!?", asked Eva while her eyes were filling with tears.

"A few days ago, I made a joke in school that involved politics, specifically, Communism. My classmate reported my remark to the Federal authorities. Do you remember Mrs. Szabo?"

"I think I do.", Eva said, "Isn't she the one that works for the investigations department?"

"Yes! Dad has known her for many, many years. She is the one who warned him about the law suit that has been filed against me".

"This is insane!", Eva scoffed, "It is ridiculous!".

"They want to send me to Siberia, Mother! I will not go! I will not go!!!", shouted Gus.

Eva looked at her son. She was astonished, shocked, it seemed like the whole world was crashing in on her.

The music stopped and the couples began going back to the tables. Gustavo took his mother back to where they had been sitting.

"So!", Istvan looked at his wife and son as they approached the table. "Did you enjoy it?" However, soon he noticed the sad shadow that was in Eva's eyes. Nothing was said at that moment. He knew now that Gustavo had told her everything. Jozsef was also coming back from the dance floor and saw that his family was getting ready to leave.

"What happened?", asked Jozsef. "Why are we leaving now? It is still early!"

"Your mother has a headache. I think the ice cream didn't agree with her." Replied his father.

Jozsef did not insist, so, even though disappointed, he followed his parents home, having no idea of the heartache his mother was suffering at that moment.

Years later, Gustavo would still clearly remember the wounded feelings of what was about to happen. Jozsef had gone out. Eva and Gus, as they used to call him, were alone in the house and she cried out all her indignation and pain.

"Why are they taking my son away from me?", Eva hugged Gus as if she could keep him by her side forever.

"Mother! Please, control yourself! Don't cry like this!", Gus begged.

Since Eva and Gus were alone at home, she cried and screamed until exhaustion. For a long time, these memories would stay with Gus, this young man, abounding with goals

4

and ideals for the future, but unfortunately, would now have to throw himself into the unknown world.

"Is she going with you?", asked Eva in a desperate manner.

"Vera?"

"Yes, that girl..."

There was a moment of silence interrupted only by the clock ticking in the living room. Eva was anxiously waiting for the answer.

"Yes, she is, mother. Isabel is also coming with us. You must understand, they are best friends."

2

The Nadasi family, together with all the Hungarians, went through immense tribulation since the year of 1944 when Hitler took over Hungary, and at that time the population counted approximately 10 million people, 10% of which were Jews.

Gustavo was born in 1931. His father was a lawyer and always provided a good standard of living for his family. When his sons were small, they used to travel to other countries such as Yugoslavia, Czechoslovakia, Austria and Italy. His wife, willing to help her husband being his secretary, had an Austrian nanny to help her take care of the boys. Because the nanny spoke German, it was easy for the kids to learn this language.

Budapest, 1938 and On

They lived in a big house surrounded by a beautiful yard filled with trees where the boys used to play after school. There was a teacher, who coincidentally was related to the family and used to take Gus to mass on Sundays. Her name was Maria. She influenced Gus' life tremendously. During the mass, she used to open a beautiful missal where, together, they would follow the whole mass sequence. When Christmas season came, Gus wrote a letter to Santa Claus and placed it on the fireplace. What an anxiety filled that little boy's heart while he waited for the day when he could open up the gifts that Santa brought. When the right moment came, everybody looked for the gifts with their names on. Gus found his gift wrapped up in colorful paper. His small fingers couldn't rip the wrapping paper fast enough. Curious eyes in the room all turned to Gus when he opened the box and shouted, "The missal! The missal that I asked Santa Claus for Christmas! It's just like the one teacher Maria has. Now, I have my own!"

One could say that the Nadasi family lived a financially stable, upper middle class life style. As a result, Gus and Jozsef attended excellent private schools. Eva, his mother, was Jewish. Gus' father's mother was also Jewish, but converted to Catholicism when she married a Catholic man. Therefore, Istvan did not have any records about himself or his family being "half Jewish". They had no idea of the immense destruction which would desolate their country and the whole Europe in a short period of time.

From 1938 to 1939, Hitler took power in Germany and started the persecution of the Jews in Europe. The news of the brutalities which were performed were almost totally concealed, however, the little information that reached the Hungarians was so horrifying that they did not believe, or rather, they chose not to believe in them. In 1942, the legislation against the Jews was approved. The first concerned marriage. It was forbidden for an "Aryan", which means "blonde with blue eyes", to marry a Jew. Additionally, Jews were not allowed to use public transportation. They were only allowed to use the last car of a train, for example, only if there were no "Aryans" that needed a place to sit in the train. Another law that was introduced was to business owners. Stores had window signs saying "We Don't Sell to Jews". All Jews were supposed to wear a yellow star, which distinguished them from everybody else.

Gradually, things were getting worse and worse. The next law was that all Jews were supposed to move into buildings whereby promiscuity was an every day scene. Twenty to thirty people had to live together in one small apartment, which was part of the famous "GHETTO".

Budapest, 1944

In 1944, Hungary was completely surrendered to Nazism. It seemed like the evil itself had taken over them. Friends and neighbors imputed Jewish families to the authorities. Those families were then forced to move to the "GHETTO", where, because of the large number of people living together, plus their belongings, etc., it was normal to see rats and cockroaches all over the place.

The deportation law was approved thereafter. Thousands of people were sent in wagons, like animals, to concentration camps where about six million innocent people from all over Europe would be assassinated.

It was quite easy for the Nazists to go into the "GHETTOS" and cowardly using guns, force the Jews to go to the concentration camps. After each "GHETTO" was emptied, it was considered "unjewished", or, in other words, free of Jews.

The Nadasi family lived in the Suburbs of Budapest, New Pest. The Government authorities also determined certain areas in New Pest as "GHETTOS". Istvan and his family were considered non-Jews because their documents indicated that they were Catholics. Istvan's mother was Jewish, but was converted to Catholicism when she met her future husband, who happened to be Catholic. Therefore, Istvan was born and raised in the Catholic religion, even though he had Jewish descendancy. Eva, his wife, had Jewish parents, but also converted to Catholicism when they met.

Gustavo and his brother, although 75% Jewish, were brought up Roman Catholics, even though they did not actually practice the religion. Because of the persecution, as a lawyer, Istvan was able to process fake documents for many Jews during the persecution, helping them to escape death during that time.

It seemed like a nightmare. A few relatives were hiding in the Nadasis' home putting them in extremely risky situation before the Government authorities. Finally, all Hungary was "ethnically cleansed", in other words "free" of Jews except in Budapest, where the "GHETTOS" were not designated. In order to get rid of the Jewish population in that area, German soldiers invaded homes where they saw the yellow star and shot entire families without asking any questions or giving them a chance to speak or defend themselves.

Gustavo at thirteen years of age was accustomed to see German soldiers lining up people along the Danube River, including women, children, and the elderly and they were all shot in the back and their bodies would fall in the water. These horrible scenes would be forever kept in Gus' memory.

Gus' maternal grandmother lived far away. The family could not contact her soon enough. They never got a hold of her and later found out that she had been sent to Auschivitz where she was assassinated in the gas chamber. This was a horrible tragedy for the Nadasi family as well as for other families who lost loved ones during the German persecution against the Jews. Gus' uncle, his mother's only brother, was a Jew and had been forced to live, together with his family, in one of the ghetto-buildings in Budapest. From that building, he was picked up by the "S.S. Commando" (a bunch of cruel and soulless Nazi soldiers), and along with all the men living in that same building, he was taken by that "Commando" to a clean-up site (from the destruction of bombings) close to Budapest for forced labor. Three days later, he was murdered by those soldiers while carrying stones and rubbles on that same site under the unspeakable cruelty and hateful supervision of those German solders. A few days later, his body was found with several broken bones, completely deformed. He left behind his wife and three young sons. All these traumas were filling Gus' heart with a strong desire to leave the country, unfortunately that was the place where his family had to live, and try to survive.

3

At the end of 1944, allied troops surrounded the country in order to win over the Germans. There were bombings going on practically every day. The population had to run to shelters as soon as they heard the siren. This was already part of the lives of Hungarians. On August 14, 1944, however, something happened which is worth mentioning. The siren was heard announcing the bombing was coming. The Nadasi family soon ran to the basement as they always did every time that happened. A few minutes later, bombs started to fall, one right after another, non-stop. First, a deafening noise was heard. After that, an explosion would take place. Each explosion would make a house tumble somewhere in the neighborhood. This particular time, however, they had the impression that their own house was destroyed for the noise heard was so intense. They were all hugging each other tightly, terrified by this whole situation they were going through. Young Gus would hold his mother's hands with all his strength to feel as if by doing this, his life would be saved. He was not brought up practicing the Catholic religion at home, but he knew that a God existed and that He would listen to people's prayers. He learned this when he used to go to mass with Maria.

The Nadasi family huddled quietly in the darkness of the basement, fearing that a bomb would explode and destroy their home. Gustavo closed his eyes and with the little that he knew about God, he begged with all his feelings and emotions, that even if they lost everything, that their lives would be spared. Gustavo kept praying for a few minutes, which for him, seemed like an eternity. All of a sudden, the siren was heard again, but this time announcing that the bombing was finished. So they all proceeded upstairs, and into a disappointing picture, a completely different world welcomed them outside. Years later, that picture would still be part of Gus' memories.

There was a full moon that night. The town had disappeared because of the bombing. The houses in the neighborhood no longer existed. All they could see was the smoky fragments that remained after the bombing. However, despite all this destruction, the only house in the neighborhood that remained standing, all cracked, with no glass on the windows, and with no roof, was the Nadasis' home. Friends and neighbors would cry together trying to console each other during that sad phenomenon of losing family members and personal belongings all at once. The Nadasi family was also crying. Eva would walk around the house like a zombie complaining about all the crystals, porcelains, and china that were found in small pieces spread all over the floor. Gus was also crying, but in his cry there was also an immense joy because his life and his loved ones were saved.

Deep inside, in his young heart, he learned that the existence of a God was true and that He listened to his prayers at that moment of affliction.

After that event took place, the Nadasi family had no choice but to move to another place while their house was being renovated. The biggest problem, however, was Eva's physical appearance, a typical brunette woman who did not hide her Jewish descent. Istvan, afraid that somebody would identify his wife as a Jew, rented a small apartment in the countryside of North Hungary, in a town called Ersekvadkert, which means "Bishop's Hunting Garden". They lived in that apartment for about three months. Their financial situation became critical. Eva reached a point where she was forced by the circumstances to exchange her jewelry for a bag of potatoes. The entire country was in a true catastrophe.

The allied troops from Russia, however, continued to move towards Hungary and brought hope to all Hungarians. The Nadasi family went back to their home, which was already fixed for them to live there. However, they had to practically live in the basement since the bombings were occurring more frequently every day. The purpose of the allied troops was to defeat the Germans. The Nadasis were already accustomed to the sound of the shooting guns, sometimes they were from miles away, sometimes they were from around their neighborhood.

Finally, after going from city to city, from block to block, all around Hungary, the Russians finally conquered the country. In New Budapest, where the Nadasi family lived, this took place precisely on the 10th of January, 1945.

Budapest, 1945

After the Germans were defeated, Communism was initiated in Hungary. The Nadasis, relieved from this entire situation, decided to go outside for a walk. The streets were covered by snow, however, they wondered why the snow was brown. That was a strange phenomenon that soon was explained. That brown color was from human blood that covered the snow laying on the streets. As the Nadasi family walked down the streets, they witnessed the dreadful scene of human legs, hands, and arms spread on the ground as well as frozen human bodies lying all over town. On this particular day, they did not see any Russian soldiers on the streets.

In spite of the circumstances that were happening at the time, deep inside the Hungarians' hearts, there was a hope of freedom expected to be brought by the Russians, but what a disappointment that was! What actually occurred was a change of ideologies. Nazism then, was replaced by Communism, which was not much different from the first one, for both preached and lived for the brutality and slavery of human beings, maybe against a different race or religion, but they were still human beings.

4

The Russians officially took over New Pest on January 10, 1945. The news was spread all over the country that there would be a "three day party" for the Russian soldiers when they could do whatever they wanted with the population. During those three days, atrocities were performed. Women were raped, jewelry and money were taken, and the Hungarians understood now that the nightmare, unfortunately, was not finished. The only thing that changed was what it was being called.

During the night, Gustavo was awakened by women's screams. The Nadasis were hoping that those three days would go by fast. Finally, it was January 14 and the Nadasi family was happy that no Russian soldier "visited" their home during the previous three days. That evening, the whole family was home and there were other relatives visiting them, including his fraternal grandmother. Around 8 p.m., they heard the doorbell. When Eva opened the door, she was surprised by the presence of seven Russian soldiers. They begin their approach by saying that the house was very nice and that wealthy people must own it. While they were saying that, they walked right into the living room where the family was gathered together. The soldiers told them that they wanted all the jewelry, watches, and everything that was valuable. Gus' cousin had warned the family about this, but Gus could not believe that the glorious Soviet army, as they called themselves, who had given them the so-called freedom from the Nazists, could act this way. Another disappointment. Gustavo watched the rude way in which the Russian soldiers took his family's most precious belongings. For years, Eva and her sister-in-law had never taken the wedding bands off their fingers, and in that moment of affliction, they could only do that by using soap and water. And so as they did, one by one, all the jewelry was surrendered to the Russian troopers who had shot guns pointing at them.

Gustavo's cousin was a beautiful 18-year-old girl, and while all this was happening, she was taking a nap in one of the bedrooms. Because of the noise going on in the living room, she woke up and still wearing a nightgown, walked straight into the living room. When the troopers saw her, they immediately took all the jewelry that she was wearing away from her, and, to complete the brutality, they took her outside where the temperature was -20°F, bare footed, where there was accumulation of snow of several days and extremely slippery.

From inside, her family and relatives could hear her desperate screams, but nothing, absolutely nothing could be done at that moment because four Russian soldiers were ready to shoot anyone that made a suspicious movement or gesture. Gustavo's uncle, the girl's father, went through the worst affliction of his whole life as he witnessed his only daughter suffer and being treated like a toy by those infantrymen.

For ten minutes, they could hear her screams coming from outside. Finally, two soldiers brought her back inside holding her by the arms and threw her on the living room floor. After that event, the entire family was locked in one of the bedrooms and the troopers started to go through all the drawers and objects around the house "selecting" whatever they wanted to take with them. Gus' uncle just kept holding his precious daughter, both of them weeping so intensively but at the same time quietly, as both were afraid for their lives. The family members could only hear the troopers talking among themselves in Russian and the noise from the furniture being moved around. This incident lasted for approximately twenty to twenty-five minutes. After that, a complete silence filled the air, as they could only hear themselves breathing, looking at each other, waiting for the person who would have the courage to move. It was only approximately two hours later that they finally opened the door and walked around the house to witness the destruction made by the Russian troopers. The furniture was ruined, all closets and drawers were left open, things were spread all over the floor, and the sofa was cut with a knife.

The Nadasis walked around the house under a heavy silence not believing what they were witnessing that day. All of a sudden, somebody noticed that the grandmother was not with them. Everybody started to look for her around the house. They finally found her inside the pantry where there was no heat. She was freezing cold and was too afraid to leave her hiding spot. It was very difficult to try and convince her that the infantrymen were gone and that she could come out. Feeling extremely traumatized, she finally stepped out.

Gustavo's cousin, still crying nervously trying to recuperate from what just happened to her, could now tell everyone what really went on while they were outside. Three soldiers wanted to rape her, but because she was screaming so loud they tried to cover her mouth with their hands. Every time they put their hands on her mouth, she bit them with all her strength several times. Finally, the Captain ordered that they stopped with whatever they were doing to her because that was already the fourth day after the "three free days" they had and they were not allowed to "party" like that anymore. That's when they brought her back inside the house and madly threw her on the living room floor. Although it was a horrible experience, the family was so relieved to find out she had not been raped, and were so proud of her for being so brave.

This was the first direct contact the Nadasi family experienced with the "glorious" troops of the former Soviet Union.

From that time forward, things became worse each day. Slowly, the process of recuperation after the war was taking place. People began to go out not being so scared anymore. Outdoor fairs were promoted, however, the currency value was going down to a point where it almost wasn't worth anything. Goods had to be paid with gold. Some products such as shoes, fabrics, clothes, etc. were being exchanged for other goods instead of money.

Little by little, the currency ("Pengo") started to circulate at an inflationary cycle with no precedents whatsoever. Never, in any other country in the world's history, was there an inflation level as the one occurring in Hungary. This economic situation was registered in the "Guinness Book of World Records" as "the greatest inflation in the Earth as of that day". This took place in Hungary between 1945 and 1947.

5

Gustavo at that time was only 14 years old and was astute enough to note the "left" tendency and communist conviction of his brother Jozsef who was 4 years older. Jozsef, about 6 to 7 months after the Russian take over, went through a surgery and had to stay in the hospital for a few days. At that time, Gustavo would hear conversations between his father and his brother who tried to convince his father about his Marxists convictions, and showing him articles that he wrote himself for a local magazine and newspaper.

Gustavo didn't understand too much about the subject for he was a little bit too young for that level of conversation, however, he would listen to what his brother had to say about his inclination and principles by which, Jozsef believed, could achieve social justice if followed through.

"The future starts here!" Jozsef used to say with excitement. "From now on, there is not going to be rich or poor because everybody can make as much money as they can produce, with no Capitalists in the middle taking advantage of the blue collar workers and paying them a lot less than what they deserve."

His father would listen to him, very patiently, and aware

of the dreams of a young man who was excited about the "blah, blah, blah's" of the Russian Communist leaders.

Gus would sit in the living room and try to do his homework, but in actuality, he could not concentrate on what he was doing for his interest at that moment was on the conversation between his father and brother.

"This first phase of the 'Great Transformation' which is now starting to take place in our country, like I told you Dad, is called Socialism", and his eyes were shining, his gestures demonstrated how excited he was just by talking about it. "After that, as a second and last phase, is complete happiness which is called Communism through which all work according to their maximum capacity and all receive according to their total needs."

Gustavo would listen very carefully to what his older brother had to say, and as time went by, Gus also started to believe that would be the answer to all social problems. He thought that everybody would live as if in the "Garden of Eden". On the other hand, something inside him would not let him fall asleep at night. His teacher, Maria, always talked about a powerful God and His Kingdom where people would go to after they die, if they believed in Jesus as their personal Savior.

Gus would act very anxiously as he waited for Sunday to come as he loved to go to mass with her. Maria, a woman with firm convictions, used to fast Sunday mornings until the mass was over. After the service, they used to go to her house for a cup of coffee, butter roll and honey. Gus appreciated those moments in his life! This was the only religious orientation he had during his childhood. He enjoyed going to mass on Sundays as well as reading the Missal which he got as a Christmas gift.

Everything became very confused in Gus' mind when he would hear his brother talk about Communism, and there was no room for God in his thoughts and beliefs. With utmost respect that Gus had for his older brother who he had as a counselor, Gus would spend hours asking questions about the subject. The main question was always the same: "Why can't I be a socialist, or communist, and believe in God at the same time?"

Jozsef patiently answered that the Communist and Socialist ideology was materialistic, and that essentially meant that it did not accept or believe in the existence of a God as the creator of universe, heaven and Earth, and everything that exists therein. Darwin's theory of evolutionism was the one adopted.

"But isn't there anybody who is Communist and a Christian at the same time?" asked Gus one more time.

"No, Guszti", and his brother would clasp his shoulders while calling his brother Gustavo by his Hungarian nickname. "There is no possibility of somebody to be a Communist and believe in God at the same time. The two things are totally opposite from one another; they don't match, understand? It is like oil and water. You could never mix those two substances. Frankly, Guszti, these religious organizations are nothing more than a few trying to explore and control the masses of people, mainly the poor."

Gustavo left his brother's room, truly disappointed. Next

Sunday, there he was with Maria, talking about the same subject. For months, this was a major conflict for young Gus. Maria's face was covered with sadness when Gus brought up the subject. She tried to explain very patiently.

"Guszti, the Communists denounce the existence of a God, but we know and are absolute certain of His existence. Although the ideas they preach seem to be attractive, unfortunately, they don't have the hope and certainty of eternal life after death, through faith in Jesus, and His sacrifice on the cross, like we do. Be determined on what you believe, even when the circumstances are adverse."

"Does that mean I could never be a Communist Christian"?

"No, Guszti, you can't. I know that you believe, like I do, in a God who is infinitely just and cares about us with love and mercy, don't you?"

Gustavo would listen very careful and look deep into her eyes as she spoke those words of wisdom.

On the way back, his head was spinning and he had a difficult time in trying to decide which position to take. After months of interviews, questions, answers and so on with his brother Jozsef and his teacher Maria, finally, Gus felt deep inside his soul that the answer to his anxiety would be to keep his religious values and fight for what he believed. He felt that God was more important to him than any political or social movement. Deep in his soul, he knew that God was and would always be present in his life. There was no political or social organization that would make him change his mind about his convictions.

6

The lives of Hungarians proceeded slowly, trying to conform to the Communist rules. The situation of the "white collar" class was gradually getting worse. Mr. Nadasi, a reputable lawyer, had no choice but to work in the legal department of a wool company, for lawyers were not needed in the Communist system. Sporadically, he would work on a divorce case, but that was not enough to keep him busy all week long. Additionally, most of his assets were confiscated for the sake of the "just cause".

Between 13 and 18 years of age, Gustavo saw very closely the injustice and atrocities committed in the name of a false idealism. He could not understand why he was not allowed to express his faith in God, or, to go to church on Sundays, which he really enjoyed.

Budapest, 1949 and On

At the age of 18, in order to be accepted in the university, Gus had to work for one year for a company that manufactured light bulbs, so he hoped he would be considered to be part of the "blue collar" category, and not "white collar", which he was at the time. Otherwise it was quite impossible to be accepted in any college or university. Even after a year of struggle, it was extremely disappointing for him to face discrimination from his colleagues and instructors because everybody knew his father was a lawyer and Gus was only trying to get away with working for that company for a year only to be accepted as if he were in the "blue collar" category.

After Gustavo was finally admitted to the university, once he began attending classes, he realized that unfortunately, most of them were completely filled with politics and ideologies of Marx, Lenin, and Stalin. Gustavo, for about 6 months, studied intensively, desperate to obtain good grades. His brother Jozsef would help him understand and memorize what had to be studied. On his final exams, however, there was a great disappointment. The teachers would ask him questions that were not part of the material required for the test. There was a systematic and continuous discrimination against him because of his family background. The teachers would ask him questions such as, "What kind of news was in the newspaper yesterday?" , or, "What happened in Italy during the elections last week?" Because of this, Gustavo could only get a passing grade in a few subjects, but not in all of them.

Due to the discrimination suffered by him, it got to the point where the school sent a student commission to his home to meet his parents. They saw the Nadasis' residence was bigger than the common house, and they also realized that Gus was not a "blue collar" individual. From this day on, he was charged a high tuition. The other students could go to school for free, but because Gus was a stranger to the blue-collar class, his father had to pay for Gus to go to school if he wanted to graduate. Gus' troubled heart would feel guilty to see his father paying such a high tuition for him to be able to attend school.

Additionally, Gustavo was often secretly interviewed by Communist party spies who would persuade him to observe and denounce his colleagues and friends who he noticed had religious feelings. By doing that, he would earn positive points on his file to help his disadvantageous position of being the son of a white-collar citizen.

Gradually, an urge for liberation developed in Gustavo's mind. "There is no human being who can be happy having to live under those circumstances where one has to hide his political or religious feelings, not being able to express his own opinion about his faith in God and above all, being obligated to denounce others that had the same political and religious convictions", Gustavo thought to himself as he tried to analyze his life and foresee what was going to happen in the future.

"No! This is not my country!" He felt deep inside that Hungary was not the place for him to live any longer. This idea of liberation was taking size and shape in his mind. The only thing he wanted was to leave the place where he felt like he was in hell and where the leaders had the intent to control the thoughts, minds and lives of each individual.

A make-up date for the exams, which Gus did not do well, was scheduled for the month of August 1951, however

Gus felt deep inside that he would not be in the country on that day.

One day, during the semester that Gus attended in school, while talking to a few buddies, he told an anti-Communist joke which made them laugh very naturally. However, somebody from that group denounced Gus to the authorities, and that's when a political lawsuit was initiated against him. He was certain that the Government was going to send him to Siberia for forced labor. Also, Mrs. Szabo, a woman who worked for the Federal police and who was friends with Istvan, told him about Gus' future being in jeopardy. Her advice was for Gus to try to escape from the lawsuit by secretly leaving the country as soon as possible.

God was already performing His plan in Gus' life. He had a friend, about the same age, who escaped from Hungary with his mother and went to Austria. At that time, they were living in Vienna. This friend of Gus' wrote him several letters telling him about his "adventure" of leaving the country, about the possibility of arriving in Austria without documents, and gave information on going overseas to countries such as U.S.A., Brazil, Canada, Australia, Argentina, etc.

They had been corresponding for some time and each time that Gus received a letter from them, he felt a desire for liberation deep inside his soul; he felt the assurance that it is possible to confront any situation in order to be able to live in a "free country" on the other side of the world.

7

Budapest, 1951

Let's go back to the year of 1951 where the narrative of these facts began.

Gustavo, a young man with his mind full of dreams, started to plan for his freedom. At nighttime, he could not fall asleep. He was too busy trying to put together pieces of this big puzzle of his young existence. Gus' feelings were hurt deep inside only to think about the fact that his own brother, even though they were so close, could denounce him to the authorities if he only knew about Gus' plan of leaving the country. That was the sad result that Jozsef suffered by accepting the Communist ideas and by being "brain washed" by those that lived for the same philosophy.

Gus would silently walk to the porch in order not to wake his family and would sit there for hours feeding his soul with the dreams of a young man seeking his own liberation.

The nights were warm and the moon was shining like a spotlight on the Nadasis' home, which once belonged to his grandparents and great-grandparents, whom Gus was thinking about while struggling with his plans to leave everything behind - his family, friends, traditions, etc.

"This can not be true!" said Gus while looking at the trees in his backyard where he remembered he used to climb while playing "hide-and-seek" with his brother. Gus' vivid blue eyes landed on the tree which he planted himself years ago. Gus was amazed to see how beautifully that olive tree grew and how nicely its shade was embracing the house.

"Now, the only two things you are missing to accomplish the three great tasks of a man in this world is to write a book and have a child!", Gus remembered the words his uncle Sandor said as he helped Gus plant that olive tree so many years ago.

"I have to forget everything. I need to be strong. I am a man now! I am twenty years old already and I can't let sentimentalism be in the middle of my plans. Liberty! Freedom! Those are the only things I have to concentrate on and think about!"

And Gus would go back to bed dreaming about his future and wondering about what was going to happen in his life.

During one of those insomnia nights, Gus remembered what his friend who lived in Vienna wrote in one of his letters. His mother, right before they left Hungary, got secretly married for she was a widow. Eva, Gus' mother, was the only one who was invited to the ceremony. Gus remembered the three beautiful roses that his mother bought to give to her friend for that special occasion.

"I just had a great idea! There is nothing more exciting than a secret marriage before a political escape!" Gustavo's imagination was flying over the facts that happened to his friend and his mother and was trying to set those facts as a reality for his own plans.

"This is incredible. It seems like I'm in the "Casablanca" movie story." However, between an idea born during the night and the fulfillment of the facts, there was a "bridge" to be built. The name of this "bridge" was Vera.

The next day, Gus was walking by where his girlfriend used to live with her aunt. While approaching her house, memories of how they met came into his romantic mind. It was at a party where a friend introduced them to each other.

This happened before he finished High School. As time had gone by, they gradually developed a strong friendship, which led them to eventually become a little bit more than just "friends".

She was the only individual available to help him perform the first part of his plans to escape the country and the only person with whom Gus felt comfortable enough to confide in. He trusted her. With that in mind, Gus ran towards her house anxious to tell her the whole story. It would take him one minute to get to her house, which for Gus, seemed like an eternity. In a few minutes, finally, the two of them were sitting under a tree by her house.

"Did something happen?" Vera would hold Gus' hand. "Is your mother still opposing to our dating"?

"No!" Gus had to breathe for a few seconds to look for the right words to explain everything to her.

"Tell me! I am getting nervous! I know something is cooking when you have that expression on your face."

"O.K.! O.K.! I'll tell you everything, but please do not interrupt me while I am telling you this." And his eyes were moving from one side to the other to ensure that nobody was around listening to the conversation.

"Do you remember what I told you last week about the political lawsuit that somebody filed against me?"

"Yes! I remember, but what is going to happen if..."

"Wait!" Gus would cordially stop her. "What happens is that because of the possibility that the Government will send me to Siberia for forced labor at the concentration camps, I made a very, very important decision." In a sad tone of voice, Gus concluded his statement: "I have to escape from the country!"

Vera's eyes in a matter of seconds were full of tears. "Are you going to leave me?"

"I am going to leave the country, Vera."

"But what about me? Gustavo looked around to make sure nobody was listening and then, he whispered, "Do you want to come with me?"

"With you?!" Her eyes became as bright as the sun.

"I am proposing to you if you want to run away from Hungary with me".

Vera dried the tears in her eyes and before Gus had the chance to say anything else, she responded in a firm tone of voice, "I will do it! I'll go with you wherever you go, even if we have to go to the moon!"

Years later, Gus would deeply regret having ever asked Vera to go with him, and he would also ask himself why he did that, but at that particular moment, he simply bombarded her with all his plans, including the secret wedding. The best date would be when his parents were out of town and that would happen in the near future. Everything would have to be done with confidentiality so that nobody would be suspicious of what they were planning to do. Only his parents knew about the lawsuit against him. If anybody else, including his brother Joszef, found out about it, the plan, without doubt, would be jeopardized, as he most likely would let the authorities know and that would cause devastating consequences for the entire family. That's why Gustavo planned the escape to take place when his parents would be away for a few days. "This way", thought Gus, "when the authorities learn about my absence and ask my parents, they can say they were out of town and don't know anything as to how it happened."

Everything was going well and they were succeeding with the plan as time went by. Before they knew or realized, they were married, not in church, but only in the City Hall. They had two witnesses, both strangers to them, and after a few routine questions, all of a sudden, they were married.

The second step to proceed with the plans was to buy maps. For a few days, they visited Vera's friend, Isabel, who said she wanted to participate in the plans and, if possible, leave the country with them as well. Even today, Gus doesn't understand exactly why Isabel wanted to go through all that trouble and danger, but the fact remained that at that point, the three friends were involved in studying maps with magnifying lenses, etc. with only one thing in mind: to escape from Communism and conquer their freedom.

The whole process took approximately three to four

weeks for they wanted to rest assured about the entire situation which they were getting into. Finally, they came to the conclusion that the borderline of Hungary with Austria, where they wanted to reach, was totally closed in and it was practically impossible to even walk near it. The borderline, known as "the iron curtain", was where the "two worlds" were being divided: the Capitalist World and the Communist World. The area surrounding the many kilometers before the border line was covered with grenades and ground mines and it was also severely monitored by the army troops. Last but not least, there was a high voltage electrical fence around that whole military area. In other words, nobody could even imagine getting close to that area.

The three friends, then, searched for another possibility and tried to find out where in the country, of all the borderlines, would have the least vigilance. They did not know if there was the same control on the border of Czechoslovakia and Austria, but anyhow, those maps were studied, "eaten", and "digested" meticulously.

They also learned of the existence of individuals who would help people bring money, or go through the borderline for whatever reason, but they would charge approximately $1,500.00 per person and that was supposed to be a "guaranteed service". Unfortunately, Gus, Vera, and Isabel could not come up with the amount of $4,500.00 for the three of them to escape all together, so they decided to handle the situation by themselves.

After a lot of research, they found an extremely small point on the map along the border of Czechoslovakia and

Austria where the Danube River divided both countries. Since they couldn't imagine electrical wires in the water and Gus considered himself a good swimmer, perhaps, they thought, that there could be a remote possibility of swimming across the river at that particular point of the border.

They continued to study the maps to find the towns which were near that location where they were thinking about swimming from. The only option available would be to cross over the border to a town in Czechoslovakia, which is another Communist country, and then from there, try to reach Austria, a free country.

8

While all these events were taking place, nobody would suspect that the three of them were planning to leave the country. Things went smooth for a few weeks until that night when the Nadasi family went to Margaret Island. While dancing with his mother, Gus whispered in her ears, in a few words, everything that was about to happen. Gus spent some time thinking about how he was going to tell his mother about his plan. It didn't take long for Gus to come up with an idea which, to him, seemed very dramatic and creative at the same time. The idea was to invite his mother to dance and then, while their spirits were involved with the rhythm of the music, a perfect ambiance before a stage of a play that was about to start: a drama about his liberation. The person who leaves, thought Gus, practically dies for the ones that stay, especially in his case who had no immediate plans to return.

After that night, Eva did everything she could to keep her son on her side and try to convince him to break away from his plans.

"Guszti, my son, listen to me, your father knows a lot of people. Perhaps, we can find a way to hide you somewhere.

This plan to take off from the country involves risking your life!" Eva embraced her son in her arms, as if he were still a baby.

"Mother, I already have decided to go forward with my plans! Don't worry, everything has been meticulously studied and calculated. I have faith in God. Everything will be alright."

"How can you expect me not to worry? You and those two maniacs will be wandering around the world and risking your lives!"

With both hands, Gus held his mother's face and delicately whispered, "Don't think of it that way. When we get to the other side, I will find a way to bring you close to me. Just don't say anything to my brother, please. You know what he is capable of doing."

Those scenes where Eva was begging for her son to stay were repeated several times. Gustavo's father didn't know what to advise him due to the gravity of the situation.

Finally, as a last resort to try and hold her son back at home, Eva invited her brother-in-law over to the house, who besides being her husband's brother, Sandor was also the family's doctor. He was short, dry, and to the point. Eva told Sandor in a few words what her son was planning to do and asked him to advise him as to what he thought was the best decision to make. To her disappointment, his answer was that they, Gus' parents, shouldn't interfere with his plans. Gus was an intelligent young man and the West side of the world was wide open for him, rich in opportunities that shouldn't be missed for anything. If Gus had an intuition about his future and destiny, nobody had the right to frustrate him in any way, much less prevent him from accomplishing his dream.

Uncle Sandor spoke slowly with conviction and it was with a voice full of emotion that he said to his nephew, "Go, Guszti. If I were young like you and if I didn't have a wife and children who I love dearly, you can be sure that I would go with you and fight to reach this "free world!"

Gus looked at his uncle with a lot of respect, thinking about how many times he would have the opportunity to be like this, so close to him.

There was a problem, however, that needed to be resolved and that was how to protect the reputation of Gus' parents before the authorities. In order not to involve them in the process of fleeing, Gus and Vera moved to a small apartment in downtown Budapest. By doing this, after they execute the plan, if for some reason the authorities would look for them, Gus' parents may contend that they were not aware of what happened to Gus and Vera since they had previously moved to their own apartment.

They lived in that apartment for more than a week and on a Friday, they began to execute their plan. They left to the north of the country along with their friend Isabel to a small town called Ipolysag located close to a stream named Ipoly which forms the border of Hungary and Czechoslovakia. They found out about the existence of this small town while studying the maps and planning for the departure. They thought this town would be ideal due to the fact that it was so small, it wouldn't call too much attention. Once they were in town, they could pretend they were college students from Budapest working on a project about that particular area. Isabel encouraged Gus and Vera to go to that town for they were afraid that somebody would find out about the truth. Isabel convinced them by saying that it would be easy to find a place to stay because in a small town like Ipolysag, there were no hotels, and they could easily knock on somebody's door and ask to stay overnight with no problem.

"How can you be so confident? What if we encounter some kind of unexpected obstacle that would prevent us from executing our plans the way we intend to?" Vera asked her friend Isabel.

"Don't worry, Vera. I already traveled this way in the past and everything worked out just fine; just like I told you." Replied Isabel.

Isabel spoke with conviction looking deep into Vera and Gus' eyes. After some hesitation on the couple's part, they finally agreed with her.

They purchased a couple of small backpacks to carry only what was extremely necessary such as toothbrushes, a few pieces of clothing, etc. They could not bring regular size luggage for they did not want to call anyone's attention. They also took their raincoats with them. They left all their documents, but were bringing only one form of I.D. Gus also decided to bring a few pieces of gold which he purchased with the money he inherited as well as a camera. Gus was wearing the watch that his father gave him on the last week.

9

Budapest, 1951

Finally, the time came. They took the train at the Budapest train station heading north to a town called Vac. That was the last town where the authorities would not ask for documents, I.D.'s, etc. From there, the three friends walked towards Ipolysag. It took them four days until they could see the town far away. Fortunately, they found a private home where they rented two rooms for two to three days. The strategy was to stay there for only the time necessary to explore the area by the river Ipoly that divided Hungary and Czechoslovakia. Time flew by while they observed the area. The width, temperature, and rapids were recorded in detail. There was some type of jungle that surrounded the area. Finally, they picked the spot where they thought was the best place for them to go in the water. It was located at a small valley full of shrubs and trees. That day, they determined an area where they would meet where they all could recognize the trees and shrubs around that particular area. From that point, the width was about 25 to 30 meters wide and that area where they were was kind of secluded where the river curved slightly.

The anxiety dominated the three friends completely. All they had to do then was wait for the friendly protective darkness of the night so that they could leave. Even though everybody in the house was asleep when they left, they had a small problem when they opened the door. The rooster started crowing when he was not supposed to; the dog got scared and started barking; Vera, Gus, and Isabel could not hold their laughter as they found themselves in such a comical situation at that point.

They started walking like three zombies, three lost shadows in the darkness of the night. The heartbeats were accelerating as they approached the valley. They finally arrived at the preset location by the river with no major problems. Gus placed his ear on the ground to hear if someone was walking nearby. Luckily, there was nobody around at that time, not even the border patrol.

"I will go first", said Isabel while fixing her backpack on her shoulders. She held on to some tree branches by the river and placed her feet in the water. "The water is not too cold", and her voice was blended with the sound of the water. Gus and Vera were next, however Vera, unlike her friend and husband, was not a good swimmer. Even though the river was not deep, in certain areas right in the middle, the necessity to swim was vital. So Gus left all his belongings by a tree, tied a rope around Vera's waist, who was wearing a life preserver, and started pulling her as he swam to the other side where Isabel was waiting for them. The only difficulty they had was that Vera's foot got caught somewhere under the water and Gus had to become a hero in order to free her foot and take her to the other side. Gus went back to get his belongings and swam back across the river with no problem.

Somewhere in Czechoslovakia, 1951

The three of them were now in Czechoslovakia. It was awfully dark and difficult in seeing where they were stepping. They did not know where to go and which direction to take. The only thing they knew from their research on the map is that if they walked in the direction perpendicular to the river, they could be certain that they would be going north. With that in mind, they started walking bare footed carrying their belongings. They walked for a while when, all of a sudden, their feet were illuminated by a flashlight. Their heart beats were briskly accelerated for they knew whom those flash lights belonged to: the border patrol. But fortunately, it was only a scary moment that they went through. Since they were bare footed just like everybody else in the region, the patrolmen thought that they were residents from the area so they did not ask any questions and just walked away. What a relief!

The three pals kept walking, silently, still trying to recuperate from that scary encounter they had a few minutes ago when they could have lost their lives in a split second if the patrol guards had only the slightest doubt of who they were or what they were doing there at that time.

It seemed like they were going so slow but Vera kept complaining that she was exhausted. However, there was no alternative or return.

"Look! There is a house up the way and the lights are on!", announced Vera while sitting on the ground. "Let's go there and ask for help."

Gus gently helped her stand up and kindly had her comprehend that it would not be prudent to act this way. They would have to keep walking until they at least reached a small town.

Finally, at dawn, they arrived at a small village where there were a few old houses and a very old church. There was no human power that could impede Vera from forgetting about the exhaustion and running towards that church. The other two friends ran after her with the hopes to find help. As the old noisy door was opened, the daylight infiltrated this archaic stone church. The only thing they could hear was their own breathing of exhaustion, breaking the absolute silence while they walked down the main aisle. They opened a door which lead them to the back room, but nobody was around.

They saw a house next door and assuming that it was the priest's house, they walked towards it without hesitating. By luck, that was in fact the priest's house who had just woken up from a cozy dream, only to drive himself into the nightmare that surrounded those three young friends.

The priest, whose name was Father Varga, was confused and his mind was going in circles as Vera described the drama in which they were involved. Even though he was surprised and scared, he decided to help them.

"We have to know how to get to Bratislava as soon as

possible" shouted Vera while holding Father Varga's hands tightly.

"Yes, my friend, yes. I understand. Please calm down and I will do everything I can to help you."

Father Varga took a map from his drawer and they had a long talk about the whole situation. Bratislava was an important city in Czechoslovakia which bordered Austria, a country located on the other side of the iron curtain. That was exactly where they needed to reach. On the West side, Hungary also bordered with Austria, but unfortunately, that location was out of question.

They could not even think about getting close to that area where the system of protection against escapes that was implemented made it practically impossible for one to think about going through the border. Land mines, explosives, high tension electrical wires, high vigilance towers, spotlights covering the whole area, infantry men carrying all types of machine guns, are only a few examples of what could be found in that border line area. Therefore, to try to escape the country from that point was totally inadvisable and impossible to happen.

At the time, the border troops were trained to simply shoot at anyone who they suspected was trying to leave the country. That was the reason why the three friends decided to go to Czechoslovakia first, which is located North of Hungary and which was also dominated by the Communism; however, they had heard that the border line control was not as severe as in Hungary. Additionally, there was a small section where the Danube River itself was the border line of Czechoslovakia and Austria, a free country.

Again, the three friends and the priest were studying the maps and the path for this adventure, enforcing even more their spirit of victory.

The plan was to get to that area where the Danube river bordered with Austria, and from that point, swim across the river to the other side. As mentioned before, that area was located very close to Bratislava, a city in Czechoslovakia. It would be physically impossible for the communists to place explosives or bombs in the river which was 500 meter wide and was intensively navigated. The main problem at that point was how to get to Bratislava.

"That's why we are asking for your help!" Gustavo anxiously stared at Father Varga. All of a sudden, his mind was filled with memories of his childhood when he used to go to church with his teacher Maria carrying the so famous missal. Father Varga reminded Gus, in a matter of seconds, of his past and at the same time, he represented an angel who would be able to help them make a practically impossible dream come true.

"Children", said the priest, "I don't want to discourage you, but Bratislava is considerably far away from here for somebody to walk there. As a matter of fact, it takes about five to six hours by train to get there."

Vera and Isabel stared at each other with disappointed looks on their faces.

"Father Varga, we don't have clothes or money to take the˙

train to Bratislava", said Gus with a strong voice, although he felt exhausted and discouraged at that moment.

"My son, this can be easily arranged. I have a lot of clothes to give to the poor. You can sort through them and pick some for yourselves. Regarding the train tickets, well..., don't worry. I will buy them for you."

Immediately, Gus opened his bag, took some pieces of gold, and placed them on the priest's hand. Father Varga however, refused them and with a smile on his face, put them back into Gus' bag.

"When I decided to become a priest, I renounced everything that would take my mind away from my ministry. Keep this, my son, you will need them. The money for the train tickets comes from an offering that was taken with the purpose of helping people with special needs, and I can not think of anybody else who needs this money more than you do". He said that while opening a box, taking some money out and then gave it all to Gus. The three of them were speechless holding hands in the silence of that beautiful sunny morning. With a voice filled with emotion, Gus whispered, "thank you..."

They quickly put on some clothes and shoes. They had a nice warm meal that the priest had prepared especially for them, and with enormous anxiety, they waited for the next day to take the first train to Bratislava. Of course they could not fall asleep for their thoughts were flying a thousand miles per hour. Also, because they had to revise their plans, they were up all night thinking of the details.

At dawn, they had a quick breakfast, again, prepared by

Father Varga, and they were ready to depart. After insisting a lot, Gus convinced Father Varga to keep his photo camera as a small token of appreciation. The priest accepted the gift saying that he could use it for church activities.

Before they left, Vera came back and took a quick look, for the last time, at the church where they stayed. There were two high towers pointing to the sky like two giant arms lifted to worship God. Vera took a deep breath, turned around and followed her fellows along a dusty road.

As Father Varga had said, the train station was not too far away, and before they knew, they were on the train en route to Bratislava. The trip was not easy. During the first few hours, only the conductor came to inspect the tickets. Isabel was not at ease. She would stand up constantly and walk from one car to the other to see if there was any type of document inspection. One time, as she took another walk through the train, she felt her heart beat stop as she saw an inspection taking place on the first car. She came back right away to advise her friends. Immediately, they proceeded to the next car and each one of them went into a lavatory room. They were very afflicted because they could not communicate with each other and they did not know where the inspectors were at that point. They stayed in the lavatory for about 10 to 15 minutes. As they opened the door, they tried to act normal when they saw each other. One by one, they proceeded back to their seats, without saying a word, almost breathless.

During the trip, they had to repeat this scene twice and walk from one car to the other in order to avoid an encounter with the inspectors. Finally, with immense relief, they saw the inspectors getting off the train. The rest of the trip was spent trying to recuperate from those frightening moments they had just gone through.

Finally, the train arrived in Bratislava. They got off the train, still dizzy and exhausted from what they had lived through the last two days and from not getting any sleep for the last two nights. However, it was impressive to see how their youth strength and strong will was helping them to go forward with their goal.

10

Bratislava, Czechoslovakia - 1951

Bratislava was an old city located outside the capital of Slovak. Its crowded streets, stores, churches, synagogues, parks, and museums made the three friends feel slightly lost. They did not know where to go or what to do exactly at that moment. They did not know where the Danube River was, how to get there, or what direction to take.

They arrived in Bratislava at 4 p.m. and went for a walk around town, but they were embarrassed to knock on somebody's door and ask for help. The sunset view took over the scene of the city and in a few minutes, it was nighttime in Bratislava. The night embraced the city and the exhaustion swept over the three fugitives. They decided to alternate their sleeping shifts. Two of them would sleep and one would stay awake looking around to make sure the other two were O.K. They would sleep in the park, in front of a museum, a building, and so on, so that they would not raise any suspicious image around the city. The best places for them to sleep were under the stairway of small buildings or behind bushes and shrubs in the parks. The only inconvenience was that those were not very comfortable places to sleep.

That particular night, however, seemed extremely long for them, but finally the morning arrived and the city was awake. Gus stretched his sore muscles from a night of broken sleep and the sun was shining on his face. He touched the girls' arms who were half asleep. "Look!, Bratislava is a beautiful city!"

The two young ladies looked at each other wondering what kind of beauty a city like Bratislava can have. After all, all cities are beautiful as long as the people who are visiting them have a cozy comfortable place to sleep and are ready to go sight seeing the next day. Then, you can say that this city is beautiful. Everything is relative - if somebody does not have a place to sleep and is afraid of his or her own shadow, then, maybe there is less beauty or attraction to be recognized.

They stood up and went for a walk. They looked at store windows comparing prices of milk, bread, and cigarettes with what they paid for those items in Hungary. Gus and Vera had a strong urge for a cigarette as they were staring at those items at the store. Isabel however, would bring them back to reality. The little money they had could only be spent on bare necessities. Their priority at that moment was to find another church and another priest who would be willing to help them. Communism and Catholicism did not match, so the only safe place they could go to ask for help would be a church.

They spent the day walking around the city trying to find a church where the three of them agreed would be a good place to knock on the door and ask for help. It was not until the next day around 9 or 10 o'clock that they unanimously elected one church to continue with their adventure. They walked in and asked somebody when the priest would be available. The priest had gone downtown and would be back later.

While they were waiting, the same exhaustion, the same discomfort took over their soul. They noticed that the church looked like the one in the small town where they came from. Everything seemed like a movie which they were watching over and over again. After about forty minutes of anxiety, the heavy church door was opened by the "angel of hope".

His physical appearance did not show more than fifty years of age, he had some hair missing and a few wrinkles on his face, which revealed that maybe he had a life of burden and distress.

In a blink of an eye, before the others approached him with any questions, Isabel asked him if he would have some free time to talk. Gus and Vera sat on the first pew without saying a word to each other, only observing both the priest and Isabel disappearing behind the altar as they walked towards the back room. They waited for almost one hour and finally they were called in to join the meeting. At that point, they had no idea how much time they would have to spend in that church.

During the meeting, they learned that their plans as they were could not be executed. Father Halmai, the priest, explained that the vigilance on the borderline was intense at that time, however there were times when the risk would not be so great. Their plan would have to be performed at the right time and there were two options for them to choose in order to wait for the right moment to escape: The first one would be for them to go back to Hungary and wait until they were told the right time to execute the plan. The second option was to hide themselves somewhere in Bratislava for an undetermined period of time so crossing over the border would be less risky.

As expected, the three of them voted unanimously to stay in Bratislava for several reasons. It would involve less risk and they would waste less time because they were already near the planned location to cross the border. Father Halmai asked them to wait in the church while he would go look for a place for them to hide.

After waiting for about one half hour, they were finally called again into the back room. Father Halmai's face conveyed peace, which was very different from his facial expression when he had first met them and heard the whole story of the three fugitives. The three friends would comment on this a few days later and agreed that he was certainly praying for God's help for them and for himself since he was taking an enormous risk by helping fugitives from another country cross the border over to Austria.

Father Halmai then showed them a big closet in one of the corners of that same room. They could stay there as long as they were quiet so that no one would know that anyone was in there. There was a bathroom right next door, which they could use when there was no one around. The arrangement was that when the conditions were plausible for them to leave, he would let them know so that they could proceed.

"Children", said Father Halmai, "I firmly believe that God sent you here so I could help you. Something similar happened to me in the past when other people helped me in Hungary and also had me hide for some time when I was being chased after for different reasons."

Vera, Isabel and Gus did not know how to thank him enough for this act of solidarity. At that moment, Gus was reminded of that night when Hungary was being bombarded and as a young boy, he held his mother's hand and prayed to God that their lives would be saved from that catastrophe. God's glorious answer, the view of the whole town knocked out with the Nadasi's house being the only one still standing in the neighborhood, made Gus leave the room quickly and locked himself in the bathroom for he did not want his friends or the priest to see him in tears of emotion that were falling on his face.

They stayed in that memorable closet for about nine long exhausting weeks in a complete critical situation, where they had to be in complete silence and only go outside at night-time, avoiding being seen by anyone.

Anabella, a middle aged lady and a friend of Father Halmai would come often to give them food and the essential things which they needed. The most important condition was that they should stay silent so no one would suspect that they were in that closet.

During those days, Anabella left a pot of food with them. After they were done with the meal, since there was no one in the church at that moment, they decided to wash the pot before returning it, as an act of appreciation. They went to the bathroom, and, before they knew, Vera dropped the pot on the floor making such a loud noise that it echoed throughout the whole church. After that incident, absolute silence took over the ambiance. They looked at each other with such fearful expressions in their faces when without any reason, they could not hold themselves and had a big laugh. At the end of this incident, the three of them were crying hysterical and hugging one another.

On the second half of the eighth week, Father Halmai told them that next week would be a perfect time for them to execute their plan. He looked at his watch; it was two o'clock in the morning, but they kept whispering just in case.

"My friends, I know somebody who I believe would be in a position to help you", Father Halmai spoke while looking in their eyes and observing their reaction. "He is a smuggler of people who want to cross the iron curtain to the 'free' side."

"That would be wonderful!" Vera held Isabel's hand, restoring the hope that was almost gone at that point.

"Yes, that would be wonderful, but the only difficulty I see is that he charges one thousand dollars per person for his services."

Frustrated, as soon as they heard those words, the three friends took a deep breath and looked at each other for a few seconds. At that moment, a decision was made. Isabel was the spokesperson for the decision which was made during that strange silent conversation among them.

"Father, we are very thankful for your intention to help and protect us during our departure to the "free world", but unfortunately we do not have that type of money to pay the smuggler. Therefore, we will proceed without his help."

Father Halmai stood up with a noticeable worried look on his face. He walked from side to side, thinking. The three friends were looking at him, anxious to find out what his decision would be. Finally he stopped and sat down again. He spoke slowly as if he were talking to children.

"I believe I can talk to this person and try to ask him if he could at least guide you through the steps, maybe he would tell you the best way or the best time to do it."

"Yes, Father! Yes! That would be fantastic!" and Gus' voice sounded kind of loud, but they were all so happy with the new possibility of freedom that nobody realized that he was talking so loud.

In a few days, the smuggler arrived to talk to the three friends and the priest. He was also young and spoke Hungarian fluently. After talking to them for a while, he drew a map showing the route they should take with all possible imaginable details.

He explained that near where they were in the suburbs of Bratislava was the Danube river, which was the border of Czechoslovakia (where Bratislava is located), and Austria, a communism-free country.

They mentioned that was the same location they chose to cross the border for that was the only spot where, after studying the maps some time ago, the Danube River itself was the border between Czechoslovakia and Austria.

"That spot", he continued, "is where tourists swim on weekends. It is an extremely picturesque and popular area.

People spend the day there picnicking and swimming. What you can see from this side of the river is a long island that is not too distant from the shore. The good swimmers usually swim back and forth until they reach the island. The swimming time should not take longer than ten to fifteen minutes. However, there are signs all over the island saying that it is a borderline zone, so it is prohibited to cross over and enter the island. Nonetheless, if somebody is able to go across the island, he or she can see the Austrian territory. From that point to Austria, the river is about five hundred meters wide. The tourists can not see Austria because the island rests right in between lands and as I said before, it is prohibited to trespass that location."

The three friends were already smiling anticipating the victory. Little by little, things became clear in their minds.

"The plan", continued the smuggler, "is as follows: You have to get there on a weekend as if you were going on vacation for a few days. You need bathing suits, some food for picnic, and of course, you understand that you have to pretend you are there to enjoy the weekend like everybody else. Do not demonstrate or show any signs of worry or anxiety. At dusk, tourists usually gather their belongings and leave. You do the same and pretend that you are preparing to leave the picnic area. However, once you leave that area, you have to meet somewhere in order to hide behind the bushes of which there are plenty and wait until it gets completely dark. Then, you have to swim to that island, but you have to be cautious and fast at the same time for it is very deep and it will probably take you about ten to fifteen minutes, as I said before. When you reach the island, you can rest a little bit and don't worry; there is nobody around. The island is completely deserted."

At that point, the young man asked the three fugitives to pay close attention to what he was about to say.

"To get to the other side of the island is very difficult. You will be going through a real wilderness area with no pre-made paths, and what I am going to tell you is extremely important: the island is very long and you have to go to the extreme end of the same where the two sides of the Danube river meet. It takes about two to three hours, depending on how fast you can walk. You have to be careful though not to walk near the water so that the night vigilance on the boats won't see you on the island. Try to walk without making any noise and do not forget that you have to walk all the way to the very end of the island where, if it were day time, you would be able to see Austria from there at a distance of approximately five hundred meters. Now, the most difficult part: It will be awfully dark, but you must go in the water right at that point on the island. You have to swim against the rapids, so you will need to use all your strength to swim faster than the rapids. If you do as I just told you, even though the water will push you far away, you will still be able to reach the Austrian territory. If you don't swim fast enough, instead of reaching the Austrian territory, you will be in Czechoslovakia again for, as I told you previously, there is a small area where the Danube River is the border line between the two countries. So, do not forget two essential, very important steps: The first one is that you must go to the very end of the island. You can not start swimming from any other point of the island for you will not arrive at the area you are supposed to arrive. The second one is that you have to swim as fast as you can so that the rapids will not take you too far from the border where you can reach the Austrian territory."

This was a fairly short meeting, however Gus, Vera, and Isabel now had a solid idea as to the direction they had to follow at a such crucial point for them to reach the freedom they so desired. They thanked the smuggler immensely for taking the time to give them all that helpful information.

11

Just as the priest told them, during the following week, the vigilance was not as strict, so the three friends were ready for that segment of the escape. They had the bathing suits ready in their backpacks, made a few sandwiches, took a few bottles of soft drinks, just like the smuggler had told them to do, in order to pretend they were mere tourists going away for the weekend. Anabella volunteered to accompany them to the picnic area, giving the impression that they were all one family spending the weekend at the "beach". This way, it would be more difficult for somebody to suspect anything.

However, those nine weeks spent inside a closet without any type of exercise, very little food, and lack of proper hygiene due to the circumstances they were living under, contributed to the way they looked when they were ready to perform the plan: they looked more like three sewer rats than three tourists. They looked in the mirror and saw bags under their eyes, but had a burning desire to survive and succeed with freedom.

It was not difficult for them to spend the day at that picnic park, for as the smuggler told them, it was a pleasant place to spend the day swimming and getting a suntan. Of course, they made the most out of that situation, trying to have fun during that day and pretending that was just a vacation day for them. Most of the times, however, the three pairs of anxious eyes were starring at the island that separated Czechoslovakia from Austria. Time seemed to be going slow, but finally, the sunset was embracing the scene. All the other tourists started to gather their belongings and prepare themselves to leave the place and return home. They did the same. The farewell time arrived, but they could not demonstrate any signs of emotion. They shook hands with the lady that helped them so much during that time. They looked deeply at each other. She smiled and murmured, "Goodbye"! They walked in opposite directions until they found a bush to hide in.

Reality is always different from a simple oral description or even from a simple imagination, but even though it was not easy, when nighttime came, the three of them were already swimming towards the island. Gus put a rope around Vera's waist and tied it to his backpack while they were swimming. Vera felt guilty for not knowing how to swim and being a "drag" for Gus, but when young, things seem not to be a "big" problem all the time. In a few minutes, the three friends were approaching the island. They sat down for a while to rest and to ensure themselves that it was dark enough to proceed. They were almost celebrating the victory at that point, for no one had seen them so far. Freedom was almost within their reach as the minutes went by.

To go across the island, however, was a lot more difficult than they imagined it would be. There was no path to follow and it seemed like a real jungle to them. Luckily, the island was not a tropical one, so there were no snakes or spiders around. Vera and Isabel got tired rather fast and were complaining that their feet hurt from stepping on branches and stones. Gus was walking in front of them trying to open up the way. He was wounded in some spots, but his desire to win was as strong as iron. Gus kept telling them that they were almost reaching the very end of the island, even though deep inside the exhaustion called for a little rest rather soon.

They kept walking and tripping their way through the dark forest. When they were half way through, Gus suggested that they rest for a while before proceeding for they still had all night to make their way through the end of the island. It was difficult for them to find a place to sit in the midst of bushes, trees, and rocks.

"I can't sit still", complained Isabel. "My whole body aches, but I really don't want to stay here doing nothing."

Vera looked at her girlfriend thinking how brave and strong she was. While massaging her own feet, Vera, as tired as she was, wondered if Isabel could at least rest for half an hour. But they could not convince her to stay there and rest for a while.

Gus and Isabel stood up and convinced Vera to continue their journey. Fortunately, it was a dark night and they looked like three shadows wandering around the island.

After walking across about three quarters of the island, the three friends felt the exhaustion in their bodies and they had no more strength to walk any further. They stopped and noted they were more than half way through the island.

"Let's go in the water!", implored Vera.

"But this is not the extreme end of the island. We have to go all the way to the end", said Gus while assisting Vera not to fall of exhaustion.

They quickly voted on what they should do at that point. The women won. They then decided to go in the water from that point on the island. The voice of the smuggler still soared in Gus' mind: "Remember, you need to go to the very end of the island...!" However, the voice of two ladies would call him to reality and he actually found that detail sort of trivial to the whole situation. He tied a rope around Vera's waist, got the backpacks ready, turned to Isabel and whispered, "We have to swim about five hundred meters, so we will alternate to pulling Vera, O.K.?"

Isabel agreed and said she was ready to go. They went in the water. The Danube River and its fearful rapids seemed to be laughing at the three friends trying to challenge it. They were in fact three strange swimmers, even though in reality only two of them knew how to swim. It was extremely dark, but they kept swimming and pulling Vera. They could only see the water around them while they were swimming; but they could not see the other side of the river. Gus turned back to take a quick glimpse at the scene behind him. The rapids were taking them away rather briskly and the island behind them looked like an express train going by at high speed. Gus hoped that the girls would not look behind for they were scared enough with the whole situation they were going through.

For a while, Gus was pulling Vera with no problem and

then, he passed the rope to Isabel so he could rest his back for a few minutes and swim freely. He swam for another five to eight minutes and when he turned around to see where his friends were, he could not see them, just the darkness around him. He tried to call them, but he could not shout for he was afraid he would call the border patrol's attention. He even took the chance to call them louder, but no response was heard. The only thing he could hear was the sound of the water trying to win over him.

Gus could not stop swimming, otherwise the rapids would take him away from his destination. Desperation took over his entire soul, his heart was full of anxiety, but he nonetheless continued to swim against the rapids. In his mind, he thought, the girls must not be too far away from him and hopefully they would keep swimming until they met on the other side of the river. However, he still had to swim for a long time and at that point, before he reached the shore, he recalled of how little time he spent near them in the water. Gus feared the worst, that the girls had not been able to swim as long as he did.

He finally made it to the other side. He remembered the words of the smuggler. He had told them about the type of vegetation they were going to find in Austria and what type of trees they would see and approximately where they were located. He advised that he had put a sign on one of the trees to ensure that they would know it was the right place, the free Austria.

Gustavo walked from side to side, but he could not see any trees around him. Still dizzy from all the swimming, he could not see anything else besides grass and weeds. The scene of the wilderness did not look like anything the smuggler had described to them. He walked from one side to the other looking for the two ladies. He thought that maybe they were laying down somewhere around there. The search was in vain. He could not find either his wife or his friend. He stopped and decided to rest until dawn. "In the morning", thought Gus, " I will be able to locate myself better and continue to look for the girls." He had no other choice at that moment.

As the sun started to rise, it was with horror that Gus realized he was right in the "iron curtain" zone. It was with great frustration that Gus found out that he was not on Austrian territory. The rapids took him a little further down and he found himself at Czechoslovakia's border with Austria, which was one of the most dangerous places to be at the time. It was with immense frustration that Gus saw a big white stone, which the smuggler described, was supposed to be between Czechoslovakia and Austria, and Gus was standing exactly on the opposite side of the "free territory".

To make things worse, he heard people's voices which were getting closer and closer. In two seconds, Gus laid down among the bushes to wait and see who was around. For a moment, his heart almost stopped beating from the shock when he realized that those people were part of the border patrol performing their daily routine of checking the area. Gus thought there were only a few soldiers by themselves and if he stayed still for a while, with some luck, nobody would notice his presence there. However, as they got closer and closer, Gus saw that the soldiers had big guns and were accompanied by big German shepherd dogs, well trained to find fugitives. Gus knew that once the dogs found somebody, they were trained to immediately kill, and the soldiers were instructed to shoot at any fugitive.

Gus lost all hope. All of a sudden, he felt an immense fear of dogs. He started sweating profusely and shaking from inside out, thinking that his life was near the end. Human beings sometimes may be deceived, but not well-trained dogs like those. Those animals could sense the presence of an individual anywhere around them, especially by the human odor, and they knew exactly how to find what they were looking for. Strangely, Gus felt more terrorized of the dogs than the soldiers themselves.

A cold sweat was coming down Gus' face. His body was completely cold and his muscles were shivering, from head to toes. He tried to murmur, "My God!", but he had lost his voice. He predicted that when one of the dogs found him, it would bark awfully loud, calling the attention of the border patrol and then it would start attacking him. If he didn't die at the animal's mercy, he certainly would be shot without being asked any questions much less given the opportunity to explain himself.

"This is the end! This is the end!". It was the only thought in his disturbed mind at that moment.

All of a sudden, the image of that horrible night he went through in Budapest with his family came back into his mind. He remembered the night of bombing when he and his family were in the basement when their lives were

in danger. He again remembered that moment when, as a young boy, he was squeezing his mother's hands in the darkness of that room. Clearly, Gus remembered how he begged God for his family's life to be protected and how God showed his mighty power. The whole town was totally destroyed and their house was the only one that remained standing. Gus could never forget the picture he saw on the night of August 14, 1944, which was now coming back to him and so real in his mind. Also, on that same night, Gus learned that he had made a friend, a friend that came from above the sky, a great friend capable of doing things that seem impossible for the human eyes.

Gus knew that only a miracle could save him from that critical situation in which he found himself. In a few minutes, while the dogs were running from one side to the other, Gus gave his life to God. At that moment, while laying there fearing for his life, Gus prayed intensively to God to execute His will in his life. He once learned that God is omnipresent and omniscient, so he prayed with all his strength for God to let him escape alive from that situation.

Even though Gus was praying with a lot of faith, he couldn't avoid the shivering of his entire body and the strong beat of his heart. There are no words that can accurately describe those critical moments of terror which Gus was going through. The soldiers were getting closer and closer and as it was inevitable, Gus saw that they let the dogs loose. The dogs started running in all directions, playing and barking. Gustavo, still in the same position on the ground, realized that one of the dogs was running in his direction.

At that moment, he closed his eyes and said: "This is it! My time has come. Please, Lord, be with me now at this arduous moment. This is the end. I surrender my life to you. Be with me Lord! Perform a miracle and if possible, spare my life! It is entirely in your hands..."

Within a few seconds, everything happened. However, to Gus it felt like an eternity. The dog inevitably noticed his presence. The dog approached him, sniffed and licked his feet and legs, and then miraculously simply walked away. The dog seemed amazingly friendly. It turned around and ran to the opposite direction. No signals or barks were given to alarm the border patrol. Gus was petrified and could not believe what had just occurred. A few minutes later, they began returning to their post and Gus could hardly hear their voices and barks as they went further and further away. The only thing he could hear was his own heartbeat.

It seemed like a nightmare! Nobody would believe it! It took Gustavo a couple of hours to recuperate from the terrorizing experience he had just gone through. He just stayed there, lying down, traumatized, dizzy, almost fainting, without being able to move. He stayed in that position for about two hours. His muscles were sore, but little by little he sat up and looked around. The protected fence separating Austria and Czechoslovakia was located about twenty meters from where he was.

All of a sudden, Gus' imagination went back to his dear teacher Maria's living room, where they were drinking tea, eating cookies, and talking about Bible stories. She told him so many stories, but there was one that came into his mind which reminded him of that scary moment he had just gone through. It was the story of Daniel being thrown to the lions. God sent his angels to shut the hungry lions' mouth and no harm was done to him, because he had faith in Him. Maria always ended the stories saying: "See, Guszti! God does things that nobody is able to do! All you need to do is trust Him and ask for His protection!" Her voice seemed so real in his memory that Gus could swear that she was right there next to him.

The miracle happened! God sent his angel and closed the dog's mouth, going in the opposite direction as if Gus was somebody he knew, and not a fugitive.

Gus' heart was filled with joy and gratitude. He then started to recuperate from the shock he had just gone through. During those intimate moments he had with God, Gus learned a new lesson of faith. God taught him to have absolute trust and faith in Him and place in his heart the certainty that He would guide him every step of the way. From that moment on, Gustavo felt like a new person; he felt secure and knew that he could make firm decisions for he was not alone - God would always be by his side.

12

When he finally stood up, Gus had a tempting idea of trying to go over the fence, which was only about twenty meters from where he was, but he soon rejected the idea for he knew that he would still have to go in the water and swim to a safe area. However, the rapids could take him to the opposite direction making things even more difficult than what they already were.

After observing the area carefully, Gus realized that the only possibility to get to the other side of the island and reach Austria would be to get to a particular location right before the borderline, where he was standing. He also realized that he made a major mistake by not walking towards the very end of the island before going in the river to swim across. Because of that, the rapids took him too far away from the point he was supposed to arrive, which was meticulously calculated by the smuggler. He laid down on the ground once more and dragged himself slowly, still afraid of being seen by the guards. Fortunately, the area was surrounded with bushes, high grass and weeds so he was able to go across without being noticed by anybody.

For many hours Gustavo walked on his hands and knees,

stopping frequently to make sure he didn't hear any noise indicating somebody's presence in the area. Everything was proceeding smoothly. Nature seemed to be helping him with its high vegetation all around.

After a few hours of walking on his hands and knees, his muscles and joints seemed like they were exploding in pain. Gustavo had wounds all over his body. Very carefully, he stood up and looked around. He noticed that he could walk standing up at that point. He continued walking and eventually saw a bridge in the distance. He walked towards the bridge and when he got really close, he noticed there were people crossing the bridge, and in fact it was somewhat crowded. He tried to clean his clothes a little bit, even though he knew was a waste of time and effort.

He approached the bridge, trying to act normal, and smiling whenever possible. He got himself in the middle of the crowd crossing the bridge over the Danube River towards Bratislava. Many people were going in the opposite direction, and Gus had the impression that they were all staring at him. He found himself face to face with police troopers, soldiers, and many others. He knew that his appearance was somewhat strange and he didn't want to call the attention of anybody. However, Gus could hear a voice coming from within that said, "The most important thing is the attitude! Cheer up!" And it was with a positive attitude that he crossed the bridge showing no nervousness whatsoever and confronting those eyes which seemed somewhat suspicious.

Even though Gus felt an immense terror coming from within, God gave him courage not to manifest his true

objective. Another concern he had was that he had no iden-
tification or any type of documentation whatsoever in his
possession, so it was natural to be apprehensive among so
many people. Fortunately, nobody asked any questions or
stopped him for any reason.

Gus walked back to the church where he had been hiding
in the closet for nine weeks. He didn't have to ask anybody.
He simply found his way back.

He went inside, walked to the back room and sat down.
Nobody was around. For a minute Gus' heart was troubled
thinking about Vera and Isabel. "Where are they? Are they
alive? How are they doing?" Everything seemed so difficult at
that moment. Gus covered his face with both hands and bent
his body over his knees, trying to recuperate his strength in
order to continue his journey.

Gus remained in that position for a long period of time
until the sound of footsteps brought him back to reality.
As soon as Father Halmai saw him, his faced turned pale.
Quickly, he closed the doors and sat beside him. His eyes
looked like two question marks. Gus told him everything,
with all details. Father Halmai looked surprised and yet,
disappointed. He said that he had no news about Vera and
Isabel.

"My son, you will only be able to try for the second time
in a week, next Saturday, using the same strategy."

"But father! You don't understand! I can't go without
Vera and Isabel. Please, let me stay here a little longer until I
find out what happened to them."

"Listen to me, son!", Father Halmai answered patiently

but firmly, "I already risked my life by letting you and your friends stay here in this church. I want you to understand my situation. I simply can not let you stay here longer than one week."

Frustrated, Gus looked at him and tried one more time: "But father, please! Think about their lives and where they might be at this moment! Perhaps they are hurt and need our help!"

"Please, don't insist. It's either your life or mine, together with the people around me." After making that statement, there was a heavy and long period of silence. Gus walked side-to-side showing his nervousness. Father Halmai put his head down and looked like he was praying. Finally, he stood up, placed his hands on Gustavo's shoulders, and looked deep in his eyes for a moment. Gustavo was going to beg him once more, but he stopped him firmly:

"What is done is history. You have no option now other than proceeding forward. God will take care of your friends. This time you will make it because you are by yourself and you don't have to worry about anybody else. Therefore, the possibility is a lot greater now, but remember two things: First, ask for God's help. Second, follow precisely the instructions of the smuggler. This time, there is no room for errors."

"But father! What if after I leave, the girls make their way back here?"

Father Halmai smiled and pointed towards the sky. "God will take care of them!"

Once again, a heavy long period of silence filled the air

and Gus walked slowly towards the door where the priest indicated to him. He reluctantly went into the familiar closet and when he saw that the door was shut behind him, he fell on the ground. His body was aching, and he could not think about anything else. He had a slight fever during that night and the next morning.

For Gus, it seemed like time during that week was dragging. He could hear the clock ticking which proved to him that time had not stopped, but everything seemed so quiet and the days were very long.

Finally, to break the monotony, in the middle of the week, Gus heard somebody opening and closing the door of the room where he was. This meant that either Father Halmai or Anabella had come in there to see him. Gus stood up, fixed his hair with his hands, and smiled when he saw the priest. Gus tried to be polite:

"I don't know if I should say 'good morning' or 'good afternoon'; I have totally lost the notion of time at this point, but..."

"My son, I have something to tell you", his voice was deep and his expression was serious.

Right away Gustavo suspected something bad had happened. The first thought that came into his mind was about Isabel and Vera. Gus looked into Father Halmai's eyes and he looked pale not knowing how to start the conversation.

"Tell me, father! Did something happen to Vera and Isabel? Do you know anything about it? Did somebody find them?"

Gus stopped for a minute and then finished the sentence he actually did not want to say: "Were they arrested?"

The priest sadly admitted that in fact that was what had happened. A shadow of discontentment covered Gus' face entirely.

"Arrested! But...are they still alive? Wounded? Please, tell me!"

"Calm down, my son. They are alive and are not hurt."

"How do you know about this? Who gave you this information?"

"The smuggler. I don't know how, but he has his own ways of obtaining information about everything that happens on the borderline. He told me that Vera, at a particular moment, let go of the rope that was keeping her close to Isabel. The rapids were too strong and she thought she was going to drown, so she got desperate and started to scream, calling Isabel's name really loud, but the rapids took them even further apart. Even though the sound of the rapids was considerable loud, her voice was heard by the border patrol who was on a boat in the area. They were both found, arrested, and taken to Györ, a city not too far from here."

"But how did this happen, father? I didn't hear anything and I know I wasn't too far away from them!"

"Well, you think you were not far away, but you actually were. The rapids dragged you to a point really far away from Vera and Isabel. The evidence of this is that you arrived at the borderline itself. They were, on the other hand, dragged much further away. You see, they were arrested by the Hungarian Patrol, which could only take place a lot further down on Hungarian territory, exactly where the Danube River becomes the border line between Hungary and Czechoslovakia."

"My God!" cried Gus. The priest hugged him for a long period of time. He let him cry to alleviate that young man's heart of so many afflictions.

They stayed in that position, hugging each other for a long time, sharing their sorrow, one of them had no strength to continue and the other felt helpless for not being able to change that sad situation.

However, as the priest had mentioned before, Gus knew that his journey had no return. He had to proceed, doing whatever it took to achieve his goal.

13

A few days later, the day to attempt his adventure one more time arrived. It was a beautiful sunny Saturday morning and as previously done, Anabella accompanied Gus to the "beach", or picnic area where they mingled with the tourists. They spent the day there until dawn, when she left him there, hiding somewhere.

Everything was going well so far. Gus felt more secure of himself and physically stronger, after all that swimming and walking he did before. However, something he didn't expect happened at that moment. When Gus was ready to swim across, a fisherman walked by the area and stayed there for a long period of time during the night. Gus had to stay in absolute silence hiding behind the bushes until finally, after what seemed like an eternity, the fisherman caught some fish and finally left the area.

Gus waited a few more minutes to make sure that the area was clear. He stood up, looked around, and went in the water. He swam towards the island that separated him from freedom. As he approached the island, he felt strangely comfortable with the area, even though he had only been there once before. He started walking while recognizing the way which was taken before, even though there was no actual "path". Gus was walking in the midst of trees, bushes, rocks, etc. He sadly smiled remembering Vera complaining that she was exhausted. When he reached the point where they had erroneously gotten into the water, Gus said to himself, "This time I will not make the same mistake. I will go until the exact location, all the way to the edge of the island. Everything is going to work out fine this time!", and he continued walking.

After a while something unexpected happened. There was a cargo boat anchored near the island. On this boat there was a dog, which naturally belonged to one of the marines, and had extremely sensitive ears. When Gus walked on the leaves and rocks on the ground, the dog would bark really loud. When Gustavo stopped, the dog would stop. This incident made Gus' journey even more difficult. Gus knew he could not call anybody's attention, therefore he took all necessary precautions to not let that happen.

Little by little the vegetation was changing from a lot of trees to fewer trees and more bushes until he reached an area where there were no bushes left; only rocks on the ground. It was a hard walk until he could reach the water. Only God knows how many times Gus fell down and got up, left with almost no strength in him to continue. In order for Gus to reach the water, he would have to walk on those rocks where the island ended. That was the exact point where he was supposed to go in the water and start swimming. It seemed like an angel was guiding him and showing him the way. At this point, Gus kneeled down on the rocks, not minding the pain on his knees and said a prayer which the priest had taught him. Feeling at ease, Gus stood up and looked at the water and its strong rapids. He tried to see the other side, but it was too dark. He had no time to waste; every minute was very precious. He went right into the water and started swimming as fast as he could. The rapids were quickly taking him down the river, but Gus didn't hesitate and didn't look back; he kept swimming and looking ahead to the "dream land", Austria. He never felt so much strength coming from within as he did at that moment. The fact that he had to swim against the rapids demanded a lot from him. All of a sudden, he realized he was saying that same prayer the priest had taught him, from the time he first put his feet in the water until that moment, constantly in his mind. Saying the prayer over and over in his head gave Gus the strength he needed to keep going. The darkness of the night surrounded him and the water was fighting against this intruder, a mysterious swimmer trying to reach the other side of the river. A burning desire to win kept him moving forward. Little by little, somewhere in the course of the five hundred meters, he felt tired. His heart was pounding hard, accelerated, his arms and legs were sore, and he was almost out of breath.

Somewhere in Austria, 1951
    All of a sudden his knee scraped something which he first thought was a fish. It was at that moment that Gus then realized that he was already on the other side of the river. He did not have to swim anymore! He could then stand up and simply walk to shore.

When one is able to stand up in the river, the rapids have no more force and the person can walk in the water. Gustavo almost screamed of happiness. He couldn't wait to get to the shore. He walked for about five or six minutes and finally stepped on dry ground. Perplexed, he looked around and noticed the vegetation around him exactly as described by the smuggler. All details such as the size of the trees confirmed that he was indeed in the right place.

Gus walked towards the trees described by the smuggler where there was supposed to be one with a mark on the trunk. He vividly searched for that tree in the dark while his heart was beating faster and faster. He had to find it! All of a sudden Gus stopped, and without belief and with awe he stared at what was before his eyes. He touched the mark of freedom! Yes! He was there! He was there indeed! The sign was deeply engraved on the trunk of that tree to help the fugitives who made it there recognize that they had reached the right place.

Gus stood there, starring at the sign engraved on that tree, trying to convince himself what was truly happening at that moment. The gates of freedom were being open before him; all he had to do was walk right in and enjoy it! After minutes of joy, Gus felt warm drops of tears rolling down his face. Little by little, the tears became a heavy cry that overflew his soul, making his body tremble as if he was washing out all the affliction that was dwelling in him for such a long time.

What a victory! He was finally in Austria! "Praise God!", said Gus. So far, that was the most wonderful event that ever happened in his life. Gus was jumping and running from side to side, bursting with happiness all around, thanking God for helping him achieve his goal. And for a long period of time Gustavo stayed there alone, celebrating his triumph over Communism and wanting to tell the whole universe about his victory and God's grace which guided him there.

After moments of emotion, Gus looked around and noticed how beautiful that place was. Even the smell of the woods and the fresh soil were somehow telling him that he was indeed in Austria. He kneeled down and let his lips touch the ground. He did it! He was a free man! A new life was waiting for him on this side of the world - a free world!

14

The beginning of the great journey was conquered, however Gus knew that he would still have a battle to fight ahead of him. The main step was taken, but that was only the beginning.

At that time, Austria was divided into four zones which were Russian, English, French, and American. Gus arrived in a free and independent country, but occupied by Russian Soviet Union military forces, therefore making it a bit dangerous.

The words of advice of the smuggler still sounded crystal clear to Gus. Because Vienna was the Federal Capital of Austria, it was also divided into four zones within itself. Gus would have to be very careful because when he reached Vienna, he would be in the Russian zone of Austria, but the safe regions within Vienna were the American, French, or English zones, not the Russian zone where he would unfortunately have to go through. Therefore, in order for him to reach one of the safe regions, he would first have to arrive in the Russian zone of Vienna, and from there, try to reach one of the safe zones.

He could not ask anybody for a ride. He would have to

walk along the Danube River for a distance of about sixty kilometers (about thirty seven miles), which would take him right into the city of Vienna.

Everything came into his mind at the same time, however Gus felt tired and decided to sleep for a while. His heart was calm and he felt asleep while thanking God for helping him achieve such a difficult task in his life. That area was very quiet, so nothing disturbed the dreams of young Gus.

He slept for a few hours. His clothes dried up and Gus opened his eyes when at dawn his face was warmed up by the sun. The birds started to sing welcoming the arrival of a new day. Gus stretched a little and felt strong enough to start walking. First, he walked along the river and after a while, he felt hungry. He looked around and didn't see any fruit trees or anything eatable. He continued walking as the morning was unfolding itself into a beautiful sunny day.

After a while, he could not bear the hunger anymore. He felt weak and unable to continue walking. "What can I eat?", Gus asked himself.

He remembered the times when his family was sitting around dinner table, talking about things that happened during the day while having a delicious hot meal. After dinner, dessert was served and they would all sit by the fireplace to spend some time together. Finally, at the end of the day, they would go to sleep, and Gus remembered his soft, warm and cozy bed. Everything seemed so far away, but he was so hungry that he could almost smell the aroma of food on the table.

All of a sudden, Gus remembered that one of his teachers

from school used to say that everything comes from nature. We are all part of nature, we can live from it and everything we need will be provided by it. While recalling this, he saw a big tree and its heavy branches almost touching the water. Having no other choice, Gus picked as many leaves as he could and ate them right there, trying to imagine that he was eating a salad with no dressing on it. The taste was bitter but the hunger took over any taste and, after a while, Gus started even enjoying it. After he had enough of those leaves, he looked at the river with its clean and fresh water. He kneeled down and drank the water from the river. He washed his face and thought to himself, "This is better than nothing."

Gus took a deep breath, fixed his backpack and continued his journey. After walking for a while, he noticed that the shore was going down in a valley so he would not be able to walk by the river. He still tried to follow the same path, but he tripped, fell, and hurt himself. All this seemed like nothing for he was so happy deep inside that everything appeared to be easy. Gus was absolute certain that God was with him. Nothing in this world would stop him from proceeding. He felt an inner strength that would impel him to continue.

Gus reached a certain point where it would actually be impossible to walk along the Danube River. Therefore, he kept walking from a distance where he could still see the river. After a few hours of walking, he could not see the river anymore and in fact became concerned of having gone too far out of the way. He totally lost his sense of direction and feared he was not on the right track. He could tell that there were people around that area, however he kept going until

he reached an area where there were some hills. Gus could see far away on one of the hills that there was some kind of red object. He walked closer to the object and finally saw a red sign with white lettering. Gus was frightened when he saw that sign. "What could that be?" The red color was the color of Communism, so for a moment Gus thought he had gone in the wrong direction and arrived at the Communist zone again.

"Why did I walk so far away from the river? Maybe I crossed a borderline during this long walk without realizing what I was doing. Oh, my God! Would this be possible?"

It seemed like a nightmare. Gus kept walking, but not with the same excitement as before. However, he needed to verify what that red sign was all about. He walked towards that red spot, getting close enough so that he could read that it said in white lettering: "SCHWEEHATER BIER". Gus started laughing at that Austrian beer advertisement. What a relief! As he looked down he saw an empty pack of cigarettes which had black lettering right in the front saying "AUSTRIA". "What a marvelous piece of garbage", he thought.

Gus just stood there for a while waiting for his heartbeat to go back to normal. He realized how weak his faith in God was; the same God that showed him His power so many times, now showed him once more that He was with him every step of the way and that he could rely completely on His infinite faithfulness.

Not too far from the beer billboard ad, Gus noticed a path which led to a house. He walked towards that house and noticed it was a small Austrian restaurant or pub where people would get together to drink beer, which was probably the product mostly sold besides food. He could actually smell the food coming from that house. Even though he was extremely hungry, Gus decided to keep walking since he would not be able to pay for the food with a few pieces of gold that he had in his backpack, and he did not want to look suspicious. Suddenly, he heard a noise from the cars on the highway nearby.

He kept walking through that narrow path, still in the woods, in the midst of trees, bushes, and several other kinds of wild vegetation, until he could actually see it. It was a fairly busy highway. Gus fixed his hair and clothes and started walking on the highway shoulder. He did not want to call anybody's attention. He remembered he had to be very careful with the Soviet Military vehicles and avoid hitchhiking.

Even though his feet were sore, Gus felt it was much better to walk there as opposed to a "jungle like" environment. He kept walking on the same highway towards Vienna. That would be a beautiful ride for somebody who is enjoying the view from inside a car, but not for Gus. The soreness on his feet was still bothering him. He could not hitchhike because nobody would stop for him anyhow, due to his appearance. His clothes were worn out, the ones he swam across the Danube River with and dried on his body.

The sun was bright and the heat was torturing young Gus. His face was burning and his feet were still sore!

However, nothing would take away the happiness he felt at that moment and the trust in God, now enhanced. He knew that every step he took would take him closer to his destination - Vienna!

He looked more like a zombie than a human being. He walked through villages and towns. At one point he couldn't take the exhaustion anymore so he took a ride on a wagon where fruits and vegetables were being transported from one town to the other. He did this a couple of times, but most of the time he walked. When he arrived at another village, he decided to stop and rest for a while for his feet were too sore. Gus was shocked when he saw that, at that point, his feet were bleeding, especially on the heels. Obviously, the sneakers he was wearing weren't that comfortable and were hurting him. The heat and the exhaustion were unbearable. He noticed a small house not too far away from where he was. He inspected the area and noticed that in the front yard of the house there was a well, so he decided to knock on the door, hoping that he could at least drink some water and wash his face and feet.

Dragging himself, Gus finally reached the door, which he knocked very weakly. He was so afraid that he actually hoped that nobody would open the door. However, in a matter of seconds, a lovely lady opened the door.

"May I help you?", asked the lady in German, which reminded Gus of his Austrian nanny.

"Yes! Would you be so kind and let me drink some water from that well? I am very thirsty and the sun is burning my face." Gus was proud of himself because he knew how to communicate in German.

Before he knew, the lady was pulling some fresh and cold

water from the well. Desperately, Gus drank a lot of water, washed his face and chest. He was so delighted that he forgot to wash the wounds on his feet.

"Thank you! God bless you, always!", and Gus kissed her hands as a sign of appreciation.

For a moment, the woman felt an impetus to pat Gus' blonde hair as she noticed the suffering that young man had been going through. But she abstained herself and waved "good bye" as Gus walked away towards the road. Gus looked back and he could hear her voice softly saying, "God be with you. God be with you!"

Gus waved back to her and glanced at the place that God provided which was a true "Oasis" in the midst of a desert of tribulation and suffering.

Even though Gus recuperated a little bit after drinking water, the exhaustion was extreme and he was practically dragging himself along the road. The signs indicated the distance to Vienna, but for him, it seemed like he was going further away as opposed to closer to his destination. He was afraid he would faint right there and consequently call somebody's attention. He saw new signs along the way and that motivated him to continue his journey.

Unfortunately, the inevitable happened. At a certain point, Gus felt he had used all of his strength and his body indeed needed to rest. He knew he still had a long way to go and that he desperately needed help. There were only two alternatives - he would have to either ask somebody for a ride to Vienna, which in this case he would be taking an enormous risk, or he could try to find a place where he could rest, wash himself, have something to eat, and sleep for a while. From the two alternatives, the second one seemed impossible to accomplish, so Gus decided to hitchhike, which was something that would go against the smuggler's recommendations.

He stopped and started waving to the cars that were passing by, except to the Russian military vehicles.

"My appearance must be pathetic since nobody stopped the car or even slowed down a little", thought Gus.

After many attempts, Gus was already losing his hopes, but all of a sudden, a young man riding a motorcycle was getting close on high speed.

Discouraged, Gus waved to him, but like the other ones, he did not stop. A few yards from there, however, he made a "U" turn and passed by Gus. He kept going the opposite direction and made another "U" turn. This time, he slowed down and stopped where Gus was standing. "Thank God somebody stopped! What a miracle!" Gus was so excited that he could hardly speak. He was staring at that young man with an indescribable look of gratitude.

He was a blonde, blue eyed Austrian man, wearing typical Austrian clothes: leather shorts and a green and white-checkered shirt. Since Gus did not say anything for a while, the man decided to ask.

"Hi! Where are you going?"

Gus recuperated from that emotional moment and told him that he was going to Vienna.

"What a coincidence! I am also going to Vienna. Would you like to ride with me?"

Gus smiled like a child. "That's exactly what I was about to ask you!"

They both laughed spontaneously and in a few moments they felt so comfortable as if they knew each other for a long time. Gus tried to get on the motorcycle. For a moment, the situation became funny as Gus had never traveled on a motorcycle before. His backpack was getting in the way and as he finally thought he was ready, he felt the seam of his shorts rip in the back as he got on the motorcycle. Gus had no choice. The safe thing to do would be to hold on to that man with both arms, but Gus had to use one hand to hold his own pants in the back.

"Hold on with two hands!", shouted the man several times. Gus however, knew that his German knowledge would not be sufficient to explain what happened, especially while riding a noisy motorcycle. What an uncomfortable situation Gus found himself in, but after all he had been through, he couldn't help but simply laugh.

It took approximately thirty minutes to arrive in Vienna. Gus could only imagine how long it would have taken him to get there on foot. The entrance to the city was somewhat different than what Gus had imagined. It was not as receptive as he thought. There was a fence and a control gate, which Gus could see from far away. Long lines of cars were being formed as they approached the city.

Gus' heart was beating so fast as he saw that the police patrol from all four occupants (U.S.A., England, France, and Russia) were asking for documents or I.D.'s. Gus realized that it wouldn't be easy to simply enter that city. If Gus were by himself, things would have been a lot more difficult, for he did not have any documents in his possession, and even if he did, how would he explain his presence there, much less the way he looked?

However, everything turned out to be like a dream. Apparently, that man on the motorcycle used to go in and out of the city almost every day, or if not, quite often. He approached a separate line of cars where they could go through the gates with no problems at all. That line was evidently for important people or for the ones who were somewhat familiar with the police troopers. It was ironic to see all those troopers in uniforms waving to them with a friendly smile. The man kindly greeted them and there they went through the city gates like kings, no questions asked.

15

Vienna, Austria - 1951

Years later these memories would still be alive in Gus' memories. Just like a dream. They went through the city gates in a blink of an eye and Gus did not want to look back as he was afraid that the dream would become a nightmare.

They kept going until they reached the suburbs of Vienna. Gustavo looked everywhere with so much joy, trying to record in his memory everything he had seen around him for that city represented the freedom he wished for so long. Everything was so perfect with the exception of the fact that Gus knew that Vera and Isabel had been arrested on the other side, the Communist side. He was confident, however, that one day they too would reach the freedom so desired by the three of them.

All of a sudden, his daydreams were interrupted by a red Viennese trolley which he had dreamed about when he was in Hungary, where the trolleys were all yellow.

The young man took him to the trolley final stop. "Where are you going?", he asked Gus with a smile on his face. "Do you have the address where you are supposed to go?"

Gustavo was shaking with emotion as he remembered

when he was in Hungary, he repeated that address so many times and memorized it, hoping that he would arrive there one day. That was the moment he was waiting for. Trying to control himself, he spoke, "I am going to Wahringer Gürtl 97/99". It seemed to him that his own voice was coming from the past like an echo and was quickly flying into the future in a blink of an eye.

"Very well! Take that second trolley across the street, do you see?"

"Yes, I see it!", answered Gus, even though everything seemed so unreal to him.

The Austrian man continued, "When you get to Kärtner Strasse, you have to change trolleys. Take the "F" trolley which will take you to the American zone where you don't have to be concerned." While he said that, he blinked one eye and whispered, "We are still in the Russian zone here, so you have to be careful! Try not to talk to anybody around here."

Surprised, Gus looked at him and wondered how that man knew he was concerned about that. Gus had not told him anything about his condition in the country or his identity, but it seemed like that Austrian man already knew everything. Gus looked at his own ripped clothes, his wounded feet, and the exhaustion probably showing on his face, all of which obviously revealed everything. Gus tried to excuse himself and explain his appearance, but the man interrupted him, "Do you have any Austrian money?"

"No, I don't". Gustavo looked down, embarrassed at the

whole situation, but the man quickly slipped his hands in his pocket, took out some money and put it in Gus' hands.

"This is enough to buy a trolley bus ticket. The same ticket can be used to take the "F" trolley. At the fourth stop, get off the trolley and walk up two blocks. Turn right, walk one block, and turn left. That is the street you are looking for."

Gustavo opened his backpack and took out some gold pieces that were still left in there and handed them to the man. His eyes began filling with tears which he tried to hide.

"Why are you giving me these things?"

"Because I believe this is probably enough to compensate for the gas you spent to bring me here and also for the bus tickets...I am sorry, but this is all I have to offer to you in return for this big favor you did for me."

The young Austrian man kindly laughed, and in a friendly manner, pushed Gus' hands away from him.

"Keep these for when you really need them", and he looked at Gus trying to encourage him. Somehow he knew the pain and suffering Gus had previously encountered.

Promptly, he got on his motorcycle, waved to Gus, and left just as quickly as when they had first met. Gus did not even have a chance to ask what his name was or to thank him one more time. Gus just stood there looking at that man on the motorcycle until he disappeared while making a turn. It seemed like a vision, like an angel that took the form of a human being and came to help him when he could no longer take the exhaustion. "Could that be an angel?", wondered

Gus. He knew, however, without a doubt that man was sent from God to help him.

Gus looked up and noticed how beautiful that day was with blue sky, no clouds. This was the sky of his freedom welcoming him together with the birds singing on the trees around him. He did it! The "Red Sea" of his life had been opened before him and he had just crossed over to the other side. He was finally able to reach the freedom which had been denied to him during so many years. He was free. He was finally free.

The trolley was ready to leave, which awoke Gus from his daydream. He got on the trolley and sat by the window. While looking out the window he saw his own reflection in the glass. It was hard to believe he was staring at his own image, it was indeed himself sitting on that Viennese "bus" which was taking him to the American zone, where "freedom" was represented. This freedom, in his mind, would be the solution to his problems. What a dreamed moment which had been vividly imagined a thousand times in his mind. Now, it was finally happening. This time, it was not a dream; it was the magnificent reality of his twenty years of existence. When everything seemed lost, God showed His power and Gus was ashamed realizing again how weak and small his faith was. He remembered this was the same God who accompanied him step by step during his long journey.

At the indicated place, Gus got off and took the "F" trolley. Everything seemed to be of a rare beauty. After a while on this ride, there was a white sign with black lettering: **"You Are Now Entering the American Zone. Welcome!"**

In front of Gus' eyes were a picture of an eagle and the American flag! The symbol of freedom! Gus was shaking from head to toe, but this time the emotion was mixed with extreme exhaustion and soreness. He finally could taste the victory which had been reached at that point. He could not hold back his tears. He cried for his victory and at the same time, for the disappointment of losing Vera and Isabel. They had been arrested and Gus felt a deep sadness about that. Those were unforgettable moments!

The trolley kept going until it arrived at the stop where Gus was supposed to get off. He felt so comfortable that he started walking as if he had lived there all his life. It seemed like somebody was taking him to the right place. With no difficulty at all, following the man's directions, he found the street he was looking for. At that point, he felt he had some fever and exhaustion, but nothing would make him stop at that moment. His eyes were wide open looking for the numbers on the houses: "129, 123, 103..., I am almost there", thought Gus.

All of a sudden, he was not able to see anything around him. Darkness surrounded him and his strength was completely gone. His body refused to take one extra step. It was inevitable. Gus fainted right there on the street. If someone saw him at that moment they would wonder: "What could have happened to that young man? What a sad condition."

16

The next day, Gus woke up in a hospital bed with many people standing around, staring at him. When he first opened his eyes, he was scared. A young man extended his arm and offered him an apple. Later Gus realized that was a generous offer since at that refugee's camp, food was very scarce.

After a few minutes, they asked Gus who he was, where he was coming from, what language he spoke, and so on. They also told him that he fainted almost in front of the camp. Somebody was walking out and saw when he fell. She notified the security guard and some other people that were standing outside. They took him inside and gave him medical assistance. They also let him sleep until that time when he woke up.

As soon as Gus mentioned that he was Hungarian, within five or ten minutes, the room was so crowded that everyone could barely fit inside. All the Hungarians that were there had a question to ask.

Gus sort of felt like an animal in the zoo. He was really confused for he did not know why he was all of a sudden the "attraction" of that place. Finally, they explained to him that it had been seven or eight months since anyone had showed up, especially from Hungary, not even people who could afford to pay one or two thousand dollars to a smuggler to help them cross the border. The situation had become worse as time went by and it was extremely dangerous as vigilance was being enforced at the borderline.

"I came here by myself without having to pay anything to a smuggler", explained Gus with almost no voice, as he was still very weak.

"Do you know what I think?", said a young man, tall, blonde, standing on the other side of the room. "He just doesn't want to tell us who helped him so that he doesn't compromise anybody. It's impossible to come to this side by oneself. I don't believe in one word he says."

That comment made people argue at that point - the ones who believed him against the ones who did not. Gus was still tired and had a severe headache. He wanted them to stop arguing, but he had no strength to ask them to calm down. They argued so much that the doctors and nurses were called and everybody was asked to leave the room.

Gus noticed one thing: whether they believed him or not, they were all celebrating his arrival in the free land, away from Communism, no matter what means he used to achieve his goal.

After everyone left the room, Gus fell asleep again. He still did not know exactly where he was, and if he was at the place he was looking for on the street before he fainted. He was extremely confused and too weak to be able to think. In any event, there he was in a hospital which rescued refugees from Communism or D. P.'s (Displaced Persons), who were people just like him.

A Jewish millionaire named Rotschild had bought the property with the intentions of helping people who ran away from Communism. However, the only requirement for the person to stay at that hospital is that the person had to be Jewish. Gus did not have any documents with him. The recommendations of the smuggler were that any type of documents could complicate matters. Gus declared himself as Jewish, in order to be able to stay there. He did not disclose that he was brought up Catholic and not Jewish.

The rest of that day was extremely refreshing for Gus' physical and emotional conditions. After sleeping those long hours, Gus was able to welcome the next day very early with a lot of energy.

The door was open and Gus saw a representative of the Camp Board of Directors who stood right in front of him.

"Good morning! Are you feeling better?"

"Yes, thank you! I only need a shower. As you can see, my feet have blood all over and wounds in a couple of spots.."

"That's fine. The bathroom is right there. We will put clean clothes for you to wear on top of this chair."

Gus was already smiling anticipating the pleasure of a warm shower.

"After you are done, they will bring you something to eat. Eat well; you need it."

Gustavo agreed with him; he couldn't wait to eat something besides tree leaves.

Before the representative left the room, he turned around as if he had forgotten something.

"Listen! After you take a shower and eat, do you think you will have the strength to be interviewed by the camp authorities?"

"Certainly! Give me about an hour and you can take me to this interview."

Gus went in the shower. His feet were still sore, but how good it felt to let the warm water fall all over his body. A soap bar never smelled so good in his life as that one did at that moment. In a few minutes, he was already wearing clean clothes. For a moment, he remembered his home, his own room, his clothes, and all his belongings he left behind. Everything was far, far away. In a few minutes, somebody walked in with cookies and fresh fruit. He ate everything with the excellent appetite of someone who hadn't eaten for a few days. Gus sat back in an armchair and thanked God for the way everything turned out to be.

In a few minutes, Gus was following somebody down the hallway of the main building. They stopped in front of a double door which was opened and Gus saw a large room with white furniture, a desk and a bookshelf. Everything was very simple and Gus was left alone in that room waiting for the "interviewers". A young man with dark hair and a middle aged lady walked into the room.

"How are you, my friend? Please, have a seat right here", she pointed to a chair right in front of the desk.

"Thank you, Frau Blum."

"How do you know my name?" she curiously smiled.

Gus pointed towards a plaque on the desk. "This is your name, isn't it?"

"Yes! And I see you are a very smart young man." She made herself comfortable on the chair and proceeded. "Are you feeling better today?"

"A lot better, thank you. I would like to take this opportunity to thank you all for everything you have done for me. You saved my life!"

The lady smiled and continued: "You were lucky that you fainted nearby. You could have died if nobody had seen you".

"Yes! I am very grateful that you helped in time!"

After explaining to Gus what kind of place he was in, she proceeded, "now, I need you to tell me everything about your escape. How did you plan all that? Why did you want to flee? Basically, I want the complete story including dates, names, and all details you can remember."

Gustavo arranged himself more comfortably in the chair and started the narrative from the time when he told the anti-communism joke in school. Frau Blum was listening to him with utmost interest and curiosity. She would interrupt him once in a while with a question, but generally she would let him talk and remember the not too distant past.

The interview lasted all day with breaks only for meals. In the afternoon, Gus started telling her about the crossing of the Danube River. He told her about his wife and Isabel. Gus noticed then that Frau Blum was somewhat disturbed. Gus continued telling her that he lost the two ladies in the middle of the river because of the rapids and noticed that part of the narrative bothered Frau Blum in such a way that Gus decreased the intensity of his detailed description of facts until his voice was lowered to a point where Ms. Blum could not hear him.

Frau Blum was crying like a child. Gustavo didn't know what to do.

"Ms. Blum, are you feeling O.K.?"

After a few minutes, she finally regained her emotions and said, "Gustavo, I don't know how you are still alive! What a terrible experience! Your wife was lost in the middle of the river with the fear to be caught by those "murderers"...yes, because they are nothing more than murderers wearing uniforms...these communists..."

Gus agreed with her and before he could respond to her remark she interrupted him, "Please come back tomorrow so we can continue the interview. This is too emotional for me. That's enough for today." Frau Blum stood up and accompanied Gus to the door. Before he left, she touched him on his shoulders and said, "I admire you, my son! Only God would give you the persistence to go on!" Gus went back to his room, waking slowly and emotionally affected by his memories.

Gus had a terrible nightmare that night. He saw Vera and Isabel swimming in the Danube, trying to hide from the border patrol. Gus was trying to help them but his hands couldn't reach up to where they were. He suddenly woke up during the night, all sweaty and nervous. He tried to calm himself down by walking to the window. When he opened it, he looked up and noticed the full moon in the sky and a lot of stars around it. He stood there, admiring the beauty and silence of the night. Little by little, he calmed down and for a moment, memories of his dear teacher Maria came into his mind. He missed the time when he used to go to her house for tea and cookies. He remembered one of those times when she took the Bible and read to him a passage from the book of Psalms.

"You see, Gus! There are millions and millions of stars in the sky...some are bigger and shine more than others, but God knows the name of each and every one of them. Isn't it incredible? That's why I always say to myself, if He takes care of nature, he will take care of me also, for I am more important than a star, a bird, or a flower - I am His child!"

Those words were still so vivid in Gus' memories that it seemed like Maria was right there next to him speaking those words. Those memories made him feel at ease. Gus was certain that God would take care of Vera and Isabel wherever they were. With that comfort in his soul, Gus was able to fall asleep again. It had been a day full of emotions, but the sun was about to rise and a new day was about to start bringing with it hope and assurance of a better future ahead of him.

The next day, after breakfast, the interview went on in Frau Blum's office until about noon. He learned then from Ms. Blum that he was not allowed to leave the camp under absolutely no circumstances during six weeks. The reason for this is that new documents needed to be prepared for him, since he did not bring any, which seemed even better in his situation, for if he had any documents with him, he would have to wait about three to four months. That was due to the fact that they had to issue legal documents from the camp and from the Austrian authorities as well.

During the six weeks, a research would be done in order to verify the veracity of names including his own name and his country of origin. Somehow, through secret means of communication, they would obtain the information from any country, even if it were behind the "iron curtain" political domain. In Gus' case, they had to find out about his background in Hungary.

On his third day at the camp, Gus had the opportunity to send a postcard to his parents. Of course, Gus had already prepared them for this and he obviously sent it under a fake name, which they already knew before hand. The card said that he was spending some pleasant days in Vienna. That would be a sign to let his parents know that he was alive and free!

It was a memorable day for his mother, Eva and for his father, Istvan. After so much agony, they finally received the good news of victory. Only two months later they were able to send Gus a letter through a friend of the family who was a diplomat and was traveling to Vienna. In that letter Gus would learn that Vera and Isabel were arrested in Gyor, which he already knew, and that they were sentenced for one and a half years in prison. They also said in the letter that after the girls were arrested, they were somehow tortured to confess if anyone else was with them, so they in fact told them that Gustavo was with them, but that he drowned in the river during the tentative crossing. The authorities sent

Gus' family a Death Certificate. Vera and Isabel did that in order to protect Gus in case he made it to the other side and they knew that he would have a long way to go. Therefore, Eva and Istvan were in fact thrilled when they received the postcard from their son. It was incredible, but the adventurous young man had crossed the iron curtain!!

17

During the first week at the camp, Gus had the opportunity to meet with his friend Ivan, who used to write to him about how he fled with his mother and now lived in Vienna. It was actually very emotional for Gus to see his friend who was the one that motivated him to leave Hungary in the first place.

Gus told him the whole story with all the details he could possibly remember. Ivan was listening to him with interest and excitement. He was very happy to hear that everything had finally worked out. Finally, when Gus told him that he had a scheduled meeting with the Rabbi in about two weeks, Ivan asked, "Guszti, you are seventy five percent Jewish, however you were not brought up Jewish, were you?"

"No, I was brought up in the Catholic religion, which was my father's religion and which my mother converted to when she married my father."

"You see, this might present a problem here. This camp is exclusive for fugitive Jews. Did you tell Frau Blum that you don't practice the Jewish religion?

"No! In Hungary somebody had alerted me to this fact, so I told her I was Jewish, which is true, however I only omitted the fact that I did not practice Judaism."

"So, listen carefully. During the meeting with the Rabbi, you will be asked to recite a few Jewish prayers in Hebrew to prove that you are in fact a Jew."

"But I don't know any Jewish prayers! And forget about saying it in Hebrew!"

"Wait! We still have two weeks before the interview, so I can teach you how to say the prayers and you just memorize them!" And the two friends laughed at their perspective to deceive the Rabbi.

From that moment until the day of the meeting, Gus concentrated only on memorizing the prayers in Hebrew. It was not easy, but his willingness to learn helped him overcome any difficulties. Ivan finally congratulated Gus the day before the interview with the Rabbi.

"It's perfect, Gus! You can deceive even the most Orthodox Jew one can find!"

The next day Gus was taken in the presence of the Rabbi. Gus thought he was an interesting character. He had long gray beard and was wearing a black gown. He actually had the exact characteristics Gus expected to see in him. He asked Gus a few questions and at the end of this somewhat quick interview, he asked him to recite a couple of Jewish prayers that he knew. Gus then said the prayers as if he were used to doing that every day of his life.

A few hours later, Gus and Ivan were laughing like two smart little boys who got away with doing something forbidden. The important thing was that Gus was accepted at the camp.

The days went by rather fast. Ivan lived with his mother

in an apartment nearby. He used to visit Gus frequently to help him overcome the anxiety of what was going to happen in his life.

In a few days, Gus received his new documents. With those in his pocket, Gus could finally go out and visit the beautiful city of Vienna.

In any event, Gus was very happy with the treatment he was receiving at the camp. He met a lot of people, some he became friends with; however, others were not so friendly. He was getting food and lodging and small amounts of money for transportation and other expenses. This was all possible due to the financial help received by American organizations through donations sent to them from the United States. He could not find work at that particular time for the unemployment rate in the country was very high, although many refugees were working in places such as factories, landscaping companies, and so on.

The new documents received were valid in Austria, including the four areas occupied by four different countries. The documents were written in four different languages namely English, French, Russian, and German which was the main language. However, those documents did not give him the legal right to work. There was a program at the camp which trained people for jobs like sewing and / or clothes alterations, landscaping, shoe making, and so on.

Gustavo was able to find a job in the "black market". He was getting paid cash for playing the piano at a small family bar that was located in the back of a restaurant. He used to play in the afternoon and at night a few days a week together with another young fellow who played the drums. That "freelance" job helped him make some extra money for his personal expenses.

Sometimes he slept over Ivan's house and they used to go sightseeing together the next day. Gus stayed at that camp for about nine months. His activity during the day was to try to obtain the immigrant visa for a country that would accept him. During a follow up interview with the camp authorities, Gus disclosed his intentions of immigrating to another country. He also told them the approximate time he needed to stay at the camp, since they all knew that his stay there was only temporary. He had to build up his future and look forward to reaching his final destiny.

Brazil was the country he chose to immigrate to. He in fact considered other possibilities such as United States, Canada, Australia, Argentina, and Venezuela. He actually always dreamed of going to the United States, the country that represented freedom and human rights, respect for life, and freedom of religion; a country that offered the possibility of a happy life, with no persecutions. Gus felt an inner gratitude for he knew that the Americans had crossed the ocean to go to Europe and fight against the Nazism and its leader, Hitler. The American freed thousands of Jews who had survived after about six million of them had been killed by the Nazists, although the ones who survived looked like walking skeletons at the concentration camps.

U.S.A. was a symbol of hope, freedom and life for a lot of people, including Gustavo. However, there were a few barriers that prevented him from going there. The main reason was that, at the time, the Korean War was taking place and the United States was involved in that war in South Korea. In order for Gus to receive the right to immigrate and legally live in the United States, he needed a relative or a close friend to sign an Affidavit sponsoring him. Unfortunately, Gus did not know anyone living in the United States at the time. His only other choice would be to volunteer to fight in the Korean War. Even though Gus had an immense desire to go to America, he didn't think it was prudent on his part to risk his life again, after all he had gone through up until then.

While he was in the process of making that decision as to where he was going to immigrate, he received a letter from his mother telling him that she had a girlfriend, Anna, who lived in Brazil. They went to high school together at the time Eva started dating her future husband. Eva said in the letter that one day, Anna and she went out for a walk with Istvan, her husband, who brought his brother Miklos along. Anna and Miklos fell in love with each other. For Anna, that was her first true love and she never forgot him. Unfortunately, they could not develop a relationship because her family was Orthodox Jewish and Istvan and his family were practicing Catholicism. They followed all the religious laws and traditions, not allowing her to marry someone who was not Jewish.

Miklos was in the Army and was studying in the Military Academy holding a high position there. He used to walk around in his uniform and the girls would go "crazy" after him. His only love, however, was for Anna. In the Army, there were also certain rules that did not allow the ones that had a higher position to go out or even be in contact with Jewish women. Due to the circumstances, that relationship was impeached forever.

When Eva wrote Anna a letter, who lived in Brazil, explaining that her son was in Vienna, Austria, and needed help to immigrate to another country, Anna answered her that she would do anything to help Gustavo, in the name of the love she felt for Miklos, Gus' uncle.

It was the year of 1952 and at that time, Anna was in her second marriage. Her first marriage was forced by her parents. She had to marry a dentist and as husband and wife they left to live in Brazil. However, they did not get along and because divorce was not legal in Brazil at that time, they got divorced in Argentina. After her first marriage was canceled, Anna married a Hungarian Jew who lived in Brazil for some time running his own optical store business adjacent to an eye doctor's office. He agreed to help Gus and was planning to start him on a career as an optician.

Gus read and reread his mother's letter with the perspective of a happy future. Gus tried to imagine himself living in South America, in a tropical country. How would that be? In any event, he knew that was a different place than the country where he was born, in all aspects. He knew that there was no snow in Brazil, the language was different, so he knew he would have to learn it, but most important of all, Brazil was a free country, away from Communism, and that fact alone was sufficient for Gus to decide to go.

In the same letter, Eva told Gus that she offered Vera

to live with her when she was released from prison, which would happen in about one year and a half. That was a relief for Gus, so at least he knew that Vera would have a place to stay.

In a few weeks, Gus received the first letter from Anna. She also sent him some money with a legal document offering to be his sponsor. She sent him a few letters from there on which expedited the emission of the immigrant visa through the Consulate of Brazil in Vienna.

The days seemed to go by quickly for Gus and he had to prepare everything for the trip rather quickly. Together with one of the letters, Anna sent Gus a ticket for him to go to Brazil by ship and told him not to worry about anything. She mentioned that she would have a place for him to stay and she would treat him as if he were her own son and they would help him build his future in the new country.

Gustavo was excited with everything that was going on. The doors were being open in front of him to enter the land of freedom. It seemed like a dream and he sometimes was afraid to wake up from that dream. It all seemed too good to be true.

After spending nine months in the Jewish camp for refugees, the day of his departure arrived. On the night before his departure, Gustavo went to visit Ivan and his mother. They had dinner together and avoided talking about his departure. Ivan's mother told them about her wedding which occurred right before her escape to Vienna.

"Guszti, your mother was the only one invited to the

wedding! We were best friends. I remember she gave me three beautiful roses as a wedding gift."

"I kind of remember; I was very little at the time, but I can still remember." Gustavo got emotional as that conversation reminded him of his mother. He looked at that lady, Rozsa, who had been friends with his mother. It seemed like yesterday when his mother was wrapping the three roses to give to her friend.

The conversation among the three friends lasted a long time, but unfortunately, the inevitable moment arrived. They had to say goodbye. They promised each other that they would keep in touch even from distant countries.

They finally hugged each other in tears, for they knew that perhaps they would not see each other ever again.

"Thank you for everything, my friends!" Gustavo tried to be strong, but he knew they were the only ones that linked him to his family and his past, and at that moment he had to let go of his emotions, separate from his dear ones, and actually only look ahead into his future. It was extremely difficult for him to say farewell, but he knew he would have to do that sooner or later.

Gustavo went back to the camp and tried to get some sleep, even though his body and mind were too excited. Finally, the important day arrived - beautiful and sunny!

Since Vienna was located in the center of the Russian zone, in order to avoid any problems, the Americans owned an "air corridor" from Vienna to Munchen, Germany, an American zone. Gustavo flew on a Pan-American Airways plane, which took him to Munchen. That route was donated to all refugees who were officially recognized as D. P.'s and lived in Vienna. The flight took about forty to forty-five minutes. It was very emotional to Gus when the airplane took off. After a few minutes, Gus had his face "glued" to the window so he would not miss any detail. The flight attendant brought lunch to the passengers. Gus looked at the plate of the person sitting next to him - baked chicken with potato salad.

"How much does it cost?" Gus asked the gentlemen.

"It does not cost anything. It is included in the price of the airplane ticket."

Gus was somewhat relieved for he did not have too much money and his flying experience was obviously limited. He had flown only twice in his life to visit his uncle Sandor.

The food tasted delicious and he would have asked for a second dish if wasn't for the fact that the airplane was arriving at the destination. At the airport there was a company car waiting for the refugees, including Gus. The car took them to Salzburg, Austria, where Gus knew Mozart was born. Salzburg was a city located in the American zone of Austria. Gustavo was amazed when he thought for a moment about the distance he had to travel to cross the Russian zone and arrive in the American zone. In any event, there he was, still in Austria. The refugees were taken to a simple hotel where they spent the night. Gus lived every second of that journey. He did not want to miss any detail of it.

Salzburg, Austria - 1952

The next day, very early in the morning, Gustavo took

the train which would take him to Genoa, Italy where the port was located. A ship called "Salta", which was part of an Argentinean company, was going to leave from that port.

The train ride was extremely long and exhausting. He left at seven o'clock in the morning. During the first few hours, the trip was going smooth. There were only a few people on the train; some were looking out the window and enjoying the beautiful view and others were sleeping in their seats. Gustavo was amazed with the beauty of the Alps. Somebody had told him before he left Austria to notice the difference in the view from Austria to Italy. When they crossed the borderline, the border officers came on the train to verify all documents, visas, etc.

The train stopped in all stations and from the first one, Gus noticed that the people who came aboard were talking loud and moving their hands quickly while they were talking. Every station stop more people would come on the train and after a while the train ride was not quiet anymore. There were a lot of people talking, and for Gus, they sounded as if they were having a fight, but at the end, they would end up laughing at something he did not understand. Gus would squeeze his body against the window and watch those people "talk". The Italian language was completely unknown for Gus and the customs were completely different than what he was used to. Gus wondered what they were talking about. After a while Gustavo understood that was the way the Italians communicated. For them, that was their natural way to talk.

The train continued on its journey. It stopped in Milan

and that train station reminded him of the Budapest and Vienna train stations, but that one was a lot bigger. They stopped there for about two hours. The passengers could get off the train, however they had to stay on the platform. Gus got off the train and took a look around at all the fruits and vegetables that people were selling at the station. Everything looked so bizarre to him. Every minute he would see somebody or something that would call his attention. Sometimes somebody would talk to him, but he didn't know how to answer them; he would only agree nodding his head.

Finally, the train departed Milan and proceeded to Venice. The passengers did not have permission to leave that station either. Gustavo felt sorry for not being able to go sightseeing in Venice, but he wanted to go by the rules so he was able to enjoy what he could see from where he was. The trip continued for another day and a half and they finally arrived in Genoa. It was about ten o'clock in the morning. Somebody from the "Joint" (the same organization from the Jewish camp in Vienna) was waiting for him to indicate the hotel where he had already made reservations.

Genoa, Italy - 1952

Gus was relieved to be able to take a shower and sleep in a warm comfortable bed. From the room he had a nice view of Genoa. He wanted to go for a long walk, but the exhaustion took over his body so he decided to stay in the room for a while, thinking and preparing himself for his new life waiting for him overseas. Looking out the window he noticed the different types of trees which he had only seen in movies, magazines, and pictures, for there are none like those in Central Europe.

In the evening, Gus came down with a cold. He thought maybe he had caught something over in Salzburg or on the train. He felt body aches, fever, and sore throat. The hotel manager offered help and he gave him some medication, different kinds of tea, but nothing really helped him feel better. Gustavo was getting anxious because he had to be at the port at ten o'clock in the morning the next day to take the "Salta" ship to Buenos Aires as a final destination, with stops in Naples, Barcelona, Canary Islands, as well as Rio de Janeiro and Santos, both located in Brazil. That ship would depart at twelve noon and Gustavo could not be even one minute late.

He tried to stay in bed resting for as long as he could, but he could not fall asleep. His thoughts were flying and he felt as if his head was spinning. He was in Europe, his place of birth, to go to another continent, America, specifically South America, not for tourism, but to start a new life in a new unknown world where the language was totally different from what he spoke. He had no idea of how his life would turn out to be from that point on. The fever was still high and he could not stop thinking about all those things at the same time. Finally he fell asleep.

At seven-thirty in the morning, he got up and did not know where to start. He put his luggage together and went downstairs for breakfast. He still had some fever and sore throat, even though the weather was warm that morning. However, he felt in "excellent" shape to travel and expected to feel better during the trip on the ship. He knew that he had to be at the port early.

"So! How are you feeling this morning?", asked the hotel manager in clear German and in a friendly manner.

"I still have fever and I feel weak."

In a matter of seconds, the hotel manager offered a glass of French cognac. "Take this and I guarantee you will feel better soon. In a few hours you won't feel a thing anymore."

Gustavo was not too excited about drinking that glass of cognac, but he decided to take a chance and he drank it in one shot. What a blessed thing that was! The drink went down his throat burning like a volcano and hot like lava. He perspired for two minutes and all of a sudden, he started to feel better.

Having recuperated his strength, Gus was able to enjoy his departure more intensively. A lot of people were traveling on that ship from many different countries such as Italy, Austria, Poland and Romania, to mention a few. There was also a large group of Orthodox Jews.

Gus had a third class ticket where people actually mingled together. Gustavo walked from one side to the other watching all those people talking at the same time in different languages. He noticed there were some Orthodox Jews. The men wore hats, had long hair on the sides, and were dressed in black. The women were wearing wigs and hats. Gus was walking around, tripping on suitcases and luggage spread all over. He also came across children sitting on portable potties which the parents brought in case of emergency. Gustavo looked around and all of a sudden he felt he was being part of a "new edition" of the Babel Tower. That whole thing affected Gus' nervous system! He was actually confused and he did not have anybody to share his feelings with.

Finally, somebody showed him where he was going to sleep and share a room with five more people, all single men: an Austrian, a Polish, and three Italians who did not quit talking day and night. After a few days, Gus got used to the sound so he could fall asleep faster, dreaming that everybody was speaking Hungarian, but he would come back to reality when it was time to wake up.

18

"SALTA" (An Argentinean Ship), 1952

When the ship started moving, people ran outside to wave farewell with white or colored cloths to the ones that were staying on shore. Gustavo tried to get a spot where he could watch that scene. Some were crying, others were screaming, and others were quiet. Gus was able to control his emotions in the midst of all those people. There were so many people saying goodbye to their loved ones and yet, nobody from his own loved ones to wave back to him. At that moment, Gus thought about his parents who loved him so much and with whom he had the privilege to stay all his life until then. He also thought about Vera and Isabel who were in prison. He remembered the good times they spent together, although they did not last long. He remembered the suffering he and his family went through during the war. All those memories made him take out a white tissue and wave to those who were staying.

"Goodbye! Farewell!" Shouted Gus in the midst of his traveling fellows. "I can't cry for leaving a place of suffering and for going in search of something better", thought Gus to himself. But our heart and emotions sometimes react differently to what reasoning can explain. Even after putting all his positive thinking and reasoning together, Gus could not avoid a few tears coming down his face.

That moment changed his emotional state for a while and it took him a few hours to recuperate. When Gustavo finally snapped out of his deep thoughts, the ship was already far into the waters of the Mediterranean. He looked around and noticed he was alone on the deck. The water was moving by fast as the ship was navigating the sea. The wind was blowing the blonde hair of young Gus who was now alone, contemplating the wonders of nature.

Gustavo slowly walked to the cabin and sat on the bed. He could feel the motion of the ship. In the beginning it was a nice sensation, but later it gave him motion sickness. He had never felt that way before. He laid down and fell in a deep sleep.

A few hours later, the Austrian man woke him up. "Come! Come and see how beautiful the view is from here!" Gus got up quickly and ran outside. He found out that the excitement was because they were arriving in Naples. The view was fabulous!

"Look! That's the Vesuvius!" shouted the young Austrian man. Gustavo had no words to answer him. It was too emotional for him and the view was spectacular. The ship arrived at the port in a few minutes. They stayed at the Naples port for about one hour and a half, therefore nobody was allowed to leave the ship. They were only letting new passengers on the ship at that point.

"I knew this place was beautiful. I had seen pictures and

post cards before, but I did not know it was this beautiful being here and seeing it live!" said Helmut, the Austrian man. Gustavo did not answer him. He would just stare at the city like a starved person looking at a plate of food, trying to feed his mind and soul with the beauty of that magnificent view.

When the ship left Naples, the whole scene of people waving goodbye to their dear ones repeated itself. This time, however, Gus did not participate in the farewell for he was more preoccupied in not missing the view of the Vesuvius and contemplating something he knew was unforgettable.

When lunch time came, they went into the cafeteria, which was a large room with long tables where several people sat together to eat. The food was native to Argentina - grilled meats, potato, salads, and what really impressed Gustavo was the big bottles of wine that were left on the table for them to drink as they pleased. The funny thing was that if they wanted water, for example, they had to order it separate, but the wine was automatically put on the table. Gustavo and his new friend Helmut could not stop eating. Everything was so appetizing and delicious.

"Where are you going", Gus asked Helmut between bites.

"I am going to Rio de Janeiro. I am a mechanic and I have a contract to work for a big company there. What about you?"

Gustavo swallowed the wine quickly and answered, "I am going to Sao Paulo. The port is located in a city called Santos. That's where I am going."

"What are you going to do there?"

"I don't know yet. I have friends who live there and are going to help me start a new life in Brazil."

They talked for a long time and Gustavo was happy that he knew how to speak German and was able to communicate with Helmut.

"You know! I am very anxious to see Spain!"

"Are we going to stop there also?", asked Gustavo in a surprised voice while wiping his mouth on a dark blue napkin.

"Not only are we going there but it will happen in a few hours. I am curious...people say it's really beautiful."

In fact, in a few hours, Gustavo and Helmut were outside in the middle of the crowd trying to see Barcelona, which was getting closer and closer to them. It was an old city which was located in such a way that the ship seemed to sail right in the middle of it, presenting a magnificent view to the passengers on board. They were able to clearly see the streets, architectural details on certain buildings, monuments, and even the people walking on the streets of Barcelona.

At that time, Franco was in power in Spain, so no one could go ashore. The ship only stopped there to obtain fuel, so they only stayed in Barcelona for about two hours. The ship then left through the Mediterranean towards to the Atlantic Ocean.

Gustavo at that point was tired so as the ship left Barcelona, he tried to get some sleep. He fell into such a deep sleep that nobody could wake him up. He even missed dinner that evening. When he woke up the next day, he had missed breakfast as well. They were already on the Atlantic Ocean! What an excitement he felt! He got up when he saw Helmut coming into the room with a tray in his hands.

"You slept a lot, my friend! You didn't have dinner, breakfast, and you missed when we went through the Gibraltar!"

"I was exhausted, Helmut. I couldn't take it anymore. But tell me! How was it?"

"It was very emotional. We had a blast! People were jumping all over the place! You missed it. You missed a great time!...Well, I brought you some fruit, bread and cookies. I didn't want to wake you up before, but I assumed you would be hungry by now."

Gustavo thanked Helmut and ate everything with an incredible appetite. He felt well rested and decided to go for a walk outside on the deck. The view was exuberant! The sun and the blue sky met far in the horizon on the Atlantic Ocean waters. That was something he had never experienced before in his life. The ocean was calm.

"Hello, Atlantic Ocean!", Gustavo greeted the ocean, getting acquainted with it. The ocean had a majestic, enormous presence. At that moment, Gustavo felt the presence of God which gave him hope and trust in the future. All his fear was gone. God was with him and he knew it!

The trip from Genoa, Italy to Santos, Brazil was estimated to be completed in fourteen days with stops in Naples, Barcelona, Las Palmas, in the Canary Islands, Rio de Janeiro, and Santos, which was Gustavo's final destination. From there the ship would continue sailing to Buenos Aires, Argentina, its final stop.

Las Palmas, 1952

When they arrived in Canary Islands, they were allowed to go ashore. Gustavo and Helmut walked around with curious eyes, checking out the whole place in detail. Las Palmas had a tropical look and people spoke Spanish there. Gustavo, who was brought up in Europe and lived there all his life, found everything in Las Palmas very primitive; he actually saw poverty there. All of a sudden, they came into a street fair. Gustavo and Helmut looked around with excitement when they saw so many bunches of bananas hanging on every tent. Since he was a little boy, Gustavo used to have bananas only as a luxury fruit, an imported item. Now cheerfully he saw the abundance of that fruit and the best part was that it was so cheap! He and Helmut shared a bunch of bananas and together they ate like two little kids having a piece of candy.

Some other passengers from the ship offered to share a taxicab to go around the island, but Gustavo and Helmut decided not to go for they wanted to walk around and enjoy that place which looked so picturesque to them.

At ten o'clock at night, they all had to be back on the ship so during the day they took the opportunity to go visit the beach. They went for a walk by the water and enjoyed the view and all the details that nature had to offer them on that beautiful island. They observed the unique vegetation and flowers. They also noticed the mountains around the city which were of volcanic origin.

Around eight o'clock, they were both exhausted so they decided to go back to the ship. They had dinner and Gustavo laid down for a while to regain his strength. The ship left at exactly ten o'clock, as scheduled, but Gus did not see the departure; he fell into a deep sleep before that time. Gustavo, once again, missed breakfast time, so when he woke up, he was very hungry. The swing of the ship made him sleep longer than normal. After he had lunch, he went outside to see the ocean. The sky was clear and the wind was blowing quite strongly.

"How beautiful!" Gustavo thought to himself. "My new life now will start at the horizon, right on that line that divides the sky the ocean. What a mystery this is! What is about to happen? Who am I about to meet? How easily and fast will I learn the language?" And Gustavo took out of his pocket a Hungarian-Portuguese dictionary that somebody gave to him and he decided to start learning a few words. He memorized how to say in Portuguese: "I am hungry", or "Please, give me food". He was laughing at his own accent and imagined how it would be when he spoke the language fluently in the land where he would be an immigrant. Later that afternoon, he felt a little bit dizzy. "I think I read too much."

However, the dizziness was increasing as time went by. He felt nausea and had headaches for the next few days. He was seasick, throwing up after eating anything. Even the smell of food made him sick. The ship was rocking too much and that made him even sicker. The trip was not too pleasant for him at that point. Other passengers also suffered from the same symptoms, but some felt it more than others. When he felt a little bit better, he went outside to his favorite spot to look out into the ocean. It was somewhat boring for all he could see was the sky and the water in all directions. The only thing that changed was the color of the water, the speed of the waves, and maybe the direction of the wind. The ocean at certain points had a dark green color and the tone would change according to the weather. Gustavo enjoyed watching those changes.

At night, the feeling was completely different. Watching the sunset every evening was something to look forward to. There was nothing that would obstruct the view of the sun at that moment. Everything confirmed the divine hands of God's creation.

Helmut and Gustavo enjoyed staying on the deck, watching the horizon and the waters being divided by the ship. Depending on the time of the day, they could see an incredible quantity of flying fish around the ship. The two friends also enjoyed the taste of salt water coming with the breeze from the ocean.

On the eighth day of the trip, the weather was extremely hot, the sky was clear, and the ocean was extremely calm. Around nine o'clock in the morning however, the captain advised the passengers through the speaker that later during the day there was a possibility of a "light" storm. He advised the passengers not to panic for that was a normal occurrence, and that the staff was well trained to handle routine storms like that. He also recommended that passengers stay in their rooms until further instructions were given.

Gustavo looked at his friend Helmut and sarcastically said, "Don't you think this captain is crazy? The weather has never been so beautiful like today! I don't see a cloud in the sky!"

And they both looked around until their eyes could reach far in the horizon in all directions. Everything looked the same - pure, deep blue sky. Everything was so calm that Gustavo did not feel sick anymore.

A few moments later, however, everything turned into chaos. Gustavo and Helmut had to stand against the wall in order not to trip over the passengers who were running and screaming after they heard the captain's warning. All of a sudden people became desperate, running up and down the stairs, and speaking in many different languages at the same time. Mothers would pull their children by the arms, who cried hysterical, terrorized with the sudden confusion. People were running from one side to the other carrying blankets and other belongings. At one point, a woman passed by where Gustavo and Helmut were, holding a cup of milk. She tripped and fell down splashing milk all over the place. There were children's bottles and other things spread all around. Gustavo looked at Helmut and thought to himself, "Did I escape from Communism to die in the midst of these people?"

At last, they decided they should go to their room. They actually had to run so that they would keep up with the movement around them. Eventually they found themselves screaming like everybody else without knowing why. The most interesting fact was that everything was happening during a beautiful, sunny day.

They finally went into their cabin, all sweaty and traumatized. They sat on the bed trying to recuperate. Gustavo looked out the round window. He could see the sky and the ocean. Everything was calm and the weather was as wonderful as before. In the corridors outside people were still running without knowing where exactly to go. That scene went on for some time and only later the passengers started to calm down.

Time went by and lunchtime came. They had not seen any storm up to that point. The two friends were kind of hungry so Gustavo suggested that they go to the lunchroom to get something to eat. Helmut agreed and in a few minutes they were both ready to go. Other people who they shared the cabin with did not understand German. When they saw that they were both getting ready to go some place, they looked at them as if they were two criminals. Gustavo and Helmut left the room quickly and quietly. When they walked into the lunchroom, there were only a few people eating there. They sat down and ate taking their time to enjoy the food and talk about various subjects.

Before returning to the cabin, they decided to walk by the deck to see what was going on up there. There was actually nobody there as people were following the captain's instructions. They decided to do the same and walked back to the cabin. It was about three o'clock in the afternoon and they kept looking outside the round window. After a while they got tired so they started talking and forgot about the storm that was about to come.

Around five o'clock the waves started moving briskly and the sky became cloudy. In a few minutes darkness surrounded them and the strong wind would bounce the ship from side to side. The waves became amazingly large, hitting the window where Gus and Helmut were. In a few minutes, the waves were gigantic. That huge ship looked like a nutshell being thrown from one side to the other. The rain started and the lightning seemed to be so close to them. The ocean was forming such large waves that they had the impression that they were going to be swallowed by them. The passengers felt like they were on a roller coaster. The strong wind, the torrential rain, the lightening, and the sudden darkness around them made that day an unforgettable one.

The two young men and all the people in their cabin were frightened, staring out the window. Some were sitting on the bed, some on the floor, some were praying, some were crying. Children were crying on their mothers' laps, who were even more scared themselves.

Gustavo looked around and wondered what was more terrifying - the storm or people's reaction. In the midst of all that, something came into his mind. That moment of terror brought him back to an incident of his childhood. One night during a thunderstorm, Gus woke up crying and his father came into his room right away. As soon as his father noticed that Gustavo was crying because he was scared of the storm, he fondly picked him up, hugged him tightly in order to make him feel secure and protected. His father told him then that he didn't have to be scared for the rain comes from God and because God is good, He would not send something for us to be afraid of. He also explained to little Gus that the storms were sent for the equilibrium of nature and also to remind us of His infinite power. Gustavo's father also explained that everything that comes from God is a blessing, so there was no need to fear because God is love.

All that came into Gustavo's mind at that moment of fear and little by little, he calmed down. He looked at Helmut and the man was clearly nervous, obviously influenced by the environment around him and all those people in the cabin. Gustavo sat down beside him and tried to appease him. He told Helmut about that episode with his father. Little by little, Helmut calmed down and stayed quiet for a while, looking at the round window, completely covered by water.

During that night the storm became worse. The ship was bouncing so much that Gustavo did not feel well. He ran to the bathroom and threw up everything he had eaten that day. To him, it seemed like he paid for all his sins right there, inside that bathroom. He came back to the cabin completely clean on the inside and according to Helmut, completely white on the outside. He collapsed in bed and fell asleep right away, even though the noise and motion from the storm would keep any person awake. He slept for many hours. It seemed like the bouncing of the ship served as a sedative to young Gus.

When Gustavo woke up the next day, the sun was shining, throwing its warm rays towards that part of the ocean which not long ago was so threatening to their lives. The sky was blue, clear, and the horizon would meet with clear green waters. He could see some fish jumping from the water around the ship. Nobody could tell how they survived the night before through that storm. That morning was one of the most beautiful ones that Gustavo had ever seen. He was amazed with the wonders of nature. For him and for all the ones that were traveling with him, that experience was a remarkable one.

Helmut also slept until late that morning. After spending some time with Gus on the deck looking out into the ocean, they felt hungry so they went to have lunch. All that motion sickness was gone with the storm.

The days went by quickly and the arrival at the "new world" was getting closer day by day. The knowledge that the arrival date was near put "butterflies" in Gustavo's stomach. There was hope and confidence mixed with uncertainty and fear of the unknown. His thoughts were constantly focused on the future with victories and failures, feelings of excitement and affliction at the same time.

From the ship, the view was always the same - the blue sky meeting the ocean far on the horizon line. Only the people's thoughts were flying faster than light speed back and forth. They all had something in common: they were counting the days left to arrive at their final destination. They all had the expectation for a new beginning, a new life, on the other side of the world. The trip on the ship represented some sort of "intermission" between the past and the future. The whole trip seemed like it made time stop and initiate a new journey - a new time, a new world. The only thing they were certain of was that they could not give up at that point. The time was coming and it was getting closer and closer each day. It was exciting! It was scary! Everything happened at the same time.

Helmut could not stop talking during these final days about the "Sugar Loaf" and the "Corcovado" which they would be able to see from the ship when arriving in Rio de Janeiro. He went to ask the captain about the exact day and time he would expect to be arriving in Brazil. He was preparing himself emotionally and getting Gustavo excited as well, who could only think about arriving in Sao Paulo where he would encounter his new beginning. Gustavo was thinking about how he would recognize the couple Pal and Anna, his mother's girlfriend from many years ago. Mr. Pal Nagy was her husband who would accompany her to the port in Santos, state of Sao Paulo.

There were only a few days left for their dream to become reality. Time seemed to go by too slow and the anxiety was increasing every second. When Gustavo was in Vienna, he bought a Portuguese grammar book and a Portuguese - German dictionary. During that time Gustavo tried to do some reading and learn some new words of the new language he would have to learn, but he was not successful. He found it too difficult to learn it by himself, but in any event, it was a good distraction for the trip. One of the phrases he learned, however, was something like "Please, give me food, I am hungry". Gustavo would show them to Helmut and together they would laugh hysterical trying to imagine how they would ask for food, like two small children asking for cookies.

Everything only served as a temporary, superficial distraction for both of them. The truth was that the anxiety deep inside took control of their thoughts and souls, anticipating their destiny. For Gustavo, who was literally counting the days, that anxiety was getting to him, making him emotionally exhausted. He didn't know what else to do to alleviate that fear of the unknown.

At night, Gustavo went to bed exhausted, lacking strength to think or imagine anything. He fell into a deep sleep when at about four-thirty in the morning, Helmut woke him up. Gustavo told him that was not an appropriate time to wake somebody up, that he was tired, and wished to sleep. Patiently, Helmut told him that if he wished to see something incredible that he had never seen in his whole life, to get up immediately and follow him up to the deck.

Rio de Janeiro, Brazil - 1952

Gustavo noticed that the engine was off and the ship was not moving. He got up at once and noticed that nobody was in the cabin. Everybody had gone out on the deck. That was a dark night. Gustavo was running through the hallways trying to go outside as soon as possible. When he was finally on the deck, he almost lost his breath. The spectacular view before his eyes was something he could not describe. He first thought he was dreaming and after pinching himself on the arm he was convinced that was pure reality. There it was, with all its beauty, the city of Rio de Janeiro, all lit up, which they could see from a perfect angle where they were and were able to appreciate the whole picture of the city. They could see the amazing gift of nature, the mountain named "Sugar Loaf". They were right by "Getulio Vargas Avenue" and the "Candelaria Church", unique in its lights

and architecture. To complete the picture, they could also see the "Corcovado" mountain, with the magnificent view of the giant sculpture of Christ, all lit up, with his open arms, symbolizing a blessed city.

Gustavo was not psychologically prepared to see all that. The view was so wide, so great, with so many lights, that for a moment Gus imagined it seemed like New Jerusalem was coming down from the sky. Gustavo felt that just for that moment in his life, everything he had gone through so far was worth doing. That was an important and glorious moment for him. God was being generous to him now after so much suffering. The beauty was so magnificent before his eyes that he could not stop looking. Helmut came nearby and asked, "So! What do you think?"

"Incredible!", answered Gustavo almost with no voice. What a privilege, he thought, to be able to be there among those people who all had the same feeling of gratefulness as he did. His emotions reached the extreme and tears started coming down his face. He wished that moment would last forever. If he were a poet, he would be able to describe everything he saw and felt at that moment. That was a dream come true. The Southern Hemisphere showing its plenitude and beauty like a precious stone with all its unique, exotic, tropical characteristics.

That was an unforgettable picture, which could have only been created by nature and by its ultimate instance, God, the creator of all nature. It was the paradise of a happy nation whose capital (which at the time was Rio de Janeiro) was so wonderful!

Gustavo would like to express all those thoughts in a poem, but in any event, there they were in any format, with no rhymes, but sincere from the bottom of his heart, where they would stay for the rest of his life!

After spending a while contemplating the view, Gustavo felt tired and went back to the cabin to lie down. He fell asleep with that beautiful picture in his mind. When he woke up, it was already daytime. The sun was shining bringing a pleasant temperature of autumn to the city of Rio de Janeiro. It was the end of May, but for Gus, it felt like Summer time for he was used to the weather in Europe, which was so much colder.

When he went back to the deck, he was able to see the same scenery, but now under the sun light which brought more life to it under the blue sky. It looked more real, more colorful. Right in the center of that scenery was the Candelaria Church, a magnificent view. The ship was still waiting for its turn to go into the port.

While he was enjoying the view, he remembered that he met a Hungarian couple in Vienna. They had gone to Brazil as well about four or five months before Gustavo did and they told him that they would be staying in Rio de Janeiro. They also told him that if the ship stopped in Rio and if the passengers were permitted to visit the city, that they would have the pleasure of waiting for him on the dock and take him for a quick tour of Copacabana. After they had left Vienna and reached their objective of arriving in Brazil as immigrants, they sent several letters to Gustavo telling how they were making out in the beginning of their new journey in South America. They also reinforced the invitation of taking him for a tour should the opportunity arise. Gustavo answered by thanking them and informing about the date of his arrival. All those things came into his mind and they seemed too good to be true. In any event, it was only a possibility at that point.

Later on, the ship started moving towards the dock. The glorious moment of stepping into the new world was really close. Gustavo was so anxious that he didn't know if he would be able to survive his emotions. Little by little, the strength and hope of twenty-one year old Gustavo helped him get over his fears. All of a sudden, they heard the announcements that anybody who was supposed to continue traveling was allowed to visit the city, but had to be back on the ship by seven o'clock in the evening.

The ship was slowly getting closer to the dock. Gustavo ran to the cabin to get his backpack. When he walked into the room, he saw Helmut preparing his luggage to leave the ship. They quietly looked at each other for a moment feeling a mixture of happiness and sadness. They didn't say anything to each other, but they both knew that it was time to say goodbye. The time they had spent traveling together on that ship allowed them to become good friends. They had many things in common which built a bond between them. They were traveling with the same purpose and objective, but they knew they were going to different destinations and sooner or later they would have to say goodbye. They promised to each other that they would keep in touch in the future and they would contact each other, even if they lived very distant from one another.

However, the fact was, that chapter in their lives was over and it was extremely difficult to say farewell. Tears came down on both their faces as they hugged each other and wished mutual happiness and luck for the present and future. They knew their destinies were different, but the opportunities were many in that "new world" they were about to step into.

The ship was getting near the dock area and the two friends ran outside to their designated lines. Helmut got on the line of the ones that were arriving at their final destination and Gustavo on the ones that would come back later and continue on to the next stop. They shook each other's hands firmly and little by little, the crowd got in between the two friends. They would wave to each other from far away, but there were so many people in between them talking so loud that in a blink of an eye, they could not see each other anymore.

The line that would take them ashore was moving quite fast going down the stairs. When Gustavo was in Vienna, somebody told him that it was very important that he stepped in the "new world" with his right foot, for that would bring him luck for the future in the new land. Even though Gustavo was not superstitious, that's exactly what he did as soon as he came down the stairs, and that he did with a lot of emotion. The first thing he felt was the tropical heat mixed with a warm breeze from the ocean.

This was the first experience he had being in the tropical weather and heat he was not used to.

19

Gustavo took his first steps on the dock following the "Exit" signs. All of a sudden, he saw a black man sitting on the steps, maybe an employee he thought, eating a banana. As hard as it is to believe, Gus had never seen anyone of the black race in his life before. Gustavo got off the line and walked towards the man and just stood there staring at him eating what seemed to be a delicious snack. Gustavo lost his sense of good behavior and politeness and was watching that man as if he had come from a different planet. Certainly, the man thought that young Gus was hungry as he saw him staring at his lunch, so he offered Gustavo some, speaking in a language that Gus could not understand. Even if Gustavo understood Portuguese, he would not understand the action coming from that man, as in Europe, people usually did not offer food to strangers. All of a sudden, Gustavo noticed that his behavior caused that man's action, so, feeling embarrassed, he ran back to the line he was following to exit the port.

Finally, he walked through a large gate. There were a reasonable number of people waiting for the passengers who had just arrived. Gustavo was looking everywhere to try to find Mr. and Mrs. Horvath, who promised to be there waiting for him. Well, to Gustavo's disappointment, they were not there. "I am not going to get upset because of that", thought Gustavo while walking towards a group of four people who did not have anybody waiting for them, like himself. They decided to venture out in the city together since they didn't have anybody to take them anywhere.

It was a beautiful sunny day, so they decided to go for a walk down the streets of Rio de Janeiro. They would often stop by store windows and curiously look inside. They reached the intersection of the Avenues Rio Branco and Getulio Vargas. They were impressed to see how wide those roads were. They waited for the traffic light to cross the street and all of a sudden they were in front of the Candelaria Church, the one they had seen from the ship, but now seen from this close distance, it gave them a total different perception of how magnificent it was.

Walking for such a long time made them tired, for after so many days on the ship, they actually were not used to walking so much, especially in a tropical weather. One lady from their group decided to go into a store to buy a pair of stockings, which caused major confusion between her and the store clerk in trying to communicate and exchange the currency. At last, everything was worked out and they left the store.

They kept walking looking all around them; the place and the people seemed so new, so unknown, yet so friendly.

All of a sudden, Gustavo heard somebody calling his name: "Guszti! Guszti!"

He couldn't believe somebody was calling his name in

a place where he didn't know anybody. He thought he was dreaming, but he heard it again! "Guszti!" He turned everywhere looking for that person calling his name when he saw far away somebody running in his direction. It was Mr. and Mrs. Horvath, the couple who promised to pick him up at the port. For some reason they were late and everybody had left the boat when they arrived. Mrs. Horvath was explaining all this to Gustavo while hugging him and bringing him in the taxicab where her husband was waiting for them. Mrs. Horvath had the idea of driving around the area taking Rio Branco Avenue as that would be the way out from the port. They actually didn't expect to find him, but they had the hope that the impossible could happen.

Gustavo didn't even have time to say goodbye to the other four people he was with. Mr. and Mrs. Horvath and Gustavo left for Copacabana, Cinelandia, and St. Clara Street, close to the intersection with Atlantic Avenue. They saw the Sugar Loaf from the car so they stopped for while to enjoy the view. Copacabana was as beautiful as a dream. They arrived at their apartment, a small place they were renting on the third floor. Gustavo was very excited with the things he had already seen and visited so far in the "new world". Even though it was close to wintertime, the whole country always offered a warm temperature which caused some kind of discomfort to people who were not used to tropical weather.

The three of them went back out to go sightseeing after eating a quick lunch in the apartment. So far Gus found Rio de Janeiro very rich in nature's gift - the ocean, the beach, the colorful umbrellas. Atlantic Avenue was unique in the sense that there were only buildings on one side of the road, the other side was the ocean, which gave a contrast to the line of buildings on the coast. The silhouette of the Sugar Loaf from far away was just astounding. On the other side was the splendor of the Corcovado looking over the city. Gustavo would pinch himself to make sure he was not dreaming.

They decided to go up on the Sugar Loaf to see the city from up there. Gustavo didn't really know how to behave before such a beautiful view. From up there they could see most of the beaches, mountains, and the city. Only God would be able to create such a jewel on this planet.

Unfortunately, time seemed to have gone by too fast and it was time to go back to the ship to continue on his journey. He kindly said farewell to the couple, thanked them immensely, and in a few minutes he was back on the "Salta" ship.

In his cabin, Gustavo laid down on his bed, exhausted, maybe not so much physically, but emotionally. He fell asleep without thinking about the next day when he would reach his final destination and when he would meet Mr. and Mrs. Nagy, his sponsors who volunteered to host him as if he were their own son. At that important moment when only a few hours separated him from that meeting, he fell into a deep sleep, trying not to think about anything. In his subconscious mind, however, everything was registering and in the middle of the night, Gustavo woke up suddenly thinking about what was about to happen.

"My God! How am I going to react? What do I do to make

a good impression to the Nagy couple? They don't even know me and they have already done so much for me! Because of them, I can visualize a brilliant, yet realistic future ahead of myself."

Gustavo rolled in bed from one side to the other. He could not stop thinking about that meeting which would mean so much to him and to his future. He tried to imagine how they looked physically: "Were they short, tall, overweight, thin? Do they still remember how to speak Hungarian?" All those thoughts were floating through his mind. Little by little, the sun started rising. Gustavo got up and started organizing his belongings, even though there was not much to gather.

20

Santos, Brazil - 1952

It was Sunday, June 1, 1952. It was almost wintertime in Brazil. The time was approaching when the important moment was about to happen. At seven thirty in the morning the ship arrived at the port of Santos and was waiting for its turn to anchor by the dock which happened around nine-thirty in the morning.

Gustavo stood in line to take the required vaccination and have his documentation checked. It was a long line and moving very slowly. There was a doctor examining people and a nurse giving the shots. Gustavo was so anxious to leave that place that he didn't even feel the pinch from the shot. When he thought he was free to go, he was disappointed to find out there was another line in which he had to stand and wait. He still had to go through customs. To him it seemed like an eternity. They only checked the two carry-on bags he had with him and the big suitcase had to stay there until the next day when he would be able to pick it up. Gustavo kept the receipt in his pocket and finally was free to walk out and go down the stairs that would take him to the dock. What a relief! Once again, he was careful enough to step on the ground with his right foot.

Excited, Gustavo started walking among those people who looked strange to him and who were talking about things he could not understand. The Nagy couple could be among those people, standing anywhere. Gustavo noticed that there were fewer people in Santos than in Rio de Janeiro. Gustavo had eye contact with as many people as he could, trying to ask if their names were Pal or Anna Nagy. He kept walking and after a while he felt sad and disappointed. Nobody was there waiting for him. Nobody was calling his name like it was written on the letters. He then decided to take public transportation to try and find the Nagy's residence which was in another city, Sao Paulo.

Gustavo thought about calculating how much money he had on him to see if he would have enough for trans-portation or even to find a place to stay, if necessary. Deep inside, however, he knew that the Nagys were around there; maybe they were late for some reason, he didn't know at that time. After thinking it over, Gustavo decided to stay inside a building and wait for a while. He found a bench and sat down for about twenty to thirty minutes.

As each person walked by, Gustavo would stare, making the situation somewhat embarrassing for those who were near him. It was not easy to take those moments of anxiety. Little by little, something came into his mind, which really made him calm down.

"God wants to show me that the world is not made out of roses", thought Gus to himself. "After being treated

148

so wonderfully by that couple in Rio de Janeiro, I have to understand that I am not in the center of the Universe and that people have more important things to do than just run after a guy at the ocean port." And there he stayed, disappointed, thinking about his life which up until then had been a valuable lesson to him.

Little by little he felt that he was having an intimate conversation with God right there, while he was sitting on that bench. Gustavo understood that God was the first one who received him in the new world. He was the one waiting for him at the port in Rio de Janeiro, before anyone else. God wanted to show him His love and remind him that He was the one who allowed him to reach his final destination of that trip.

"God has helped until now!", thought young Gus with a lot of faith and hope. "He would not have permitted that I arrived here in this country if He did not have a plan for my life", and that would comfort Gustavo immensely. He felt so strong that he was committed to fight for his future with or without the Nagys. Gustavo was sure that those were the emotions that God wanted him to feel at that moment. Gustavo felt an immense strength coming from within and all of a sudden, he heard voices calling his name.

"Guszti! Guszti!", somebody was calling his name. He turned, still not believing what he was hearing. He stood up at once when he saw the Nagys running towards him. It was an unforgettable moment. They hugged each other for a long period of time. Anna would call him, "Gusztikam!,

Gusztikam!", which means, "My little Gus! My little Gus!....
Were you waiting for a long time?"

"No, not at all, only for a little while!", and Gustavo looked
at them, finally seeing who he was so anxiously waiting for.

Mrs. Nagy looked like she was in her fifties. She was tall,
had dark eyes and hair, and was a little overweight. She had
a strong deep voice compared to other women's voices. She
seemed to have a strong personality. Gustavo looked at them
trying to record in his memory that moment which meant
so much to him. He also noticed how elegant she looked,
wearing a brown and green suit, brown shoes which she
mentioned later she had bought in Argentina.

Mr. Nagy was somewhat short and looked like he was in
his sixties. He had gray hair, blue eyes and was also dressed
very elegantly in a casual suit and white shirt.

"Welcome to the blessed land! Welcome to our family!",
said Anna while hugging him and making him turn around
so that she could see him from all angles. Mr. Nagy also
hugged Gustavo and welcomed him.

"Guszti", said Mr. Nagy, "I want you to forgive us for
arriving here so late. We spent the night in our condo here in
Santos. Yesterday, we called to confirm the schedule of your
arrival. I think there was a misunderstanding because the
ship you were on is called "Salta", and there was another one
called "Malta", which also arrived today, but later than yours.
They gave us the schedule of the second ship, Malta, which
obviously was not the one you were on. I actually wanted to
come here following the schedule you gave us in the letter
you wrote, but Anna is so stubborn and did not want to

come earlier. She believed what the port information service told us, so she didn't want to come here and wait until three o'clock in the afternoon sitting on these uncomfortable seats."

"Guszti!", replied Anna trying to excuse herself, "It's not my fault that those people gave us the wrong information. Actually we came over only a little bit late."

"Well! That's because I insisted. You actually wanted to come at three o'clock", replied Mr. Nagy politely but firmly to his wife.

"Guszti! We were so nervous when we got to the arrival location and realized that it was all a misunderstanding. All the passengers had already left." Anna held Gustavo's hand, trying to excuse herself for what had happened. "We tried to go through a different gate and we walked around calling your name out loud. We went to different rooms to look for you but we couldn't find you. Pal kept telling me that it was my fault!"

"But it is!", interrupted Pal. "I got really nervous with the whole situation. The only thing I could think about was to find Guszti. I would ask myself, maybe he is outside walking through the streets without knowing where to go, with no knowledge of the language, and without knowing which direction to take! And everything because of her! I would have to be the one going around town like crazy trying to find you."

Gustavo soon noticed that the couple was arguing because of him and that whole situation. It seemed like the argument would go on forever. He then put his arms around both of them and gently said, "Look! I don't want you to argue over me. I want to be a reason for joy and not arguments or misunderstanding. My presence here overcomes any difficulties that might have happened, therefore there is no reason to be upset now. Let's celebrate!"

All of a sudden, the three of them were laughing together while leaving the place hugging each other, happy and talkative like three old friends who hadn't seen each other for a long time.

For a moment, Gustavo turned around and contemplated the big ship that brought him over from so far away. He imagined himself as a butterfly coming out of the cocoon. He felt like the most beautiful and colorful butterfly, ready to fly, full of life flying out in the world after so much time getting ready and being prepared for it.

It was almost one year ago that he was looking at maps, imagining what to do to escape from the prison of Communism into the free world. Now, here he was, reaching the reality that was once a dream. The new world was opening its wide gates for him to not only walk through, but also to fly into his new life of freedom, using the wings of courage, optimism, trust in God and hope for the future.

Gustavo waved to the ship. He then turned back to the Nagy couple who were observing him silently, with a lot of respect, for they understood how emotional that moment was for Gustavo. They hugged once more and continued walking.

The day was bright, sunny, the sky was deep blue, showing the tropical climate of the country which welcomed him as a son, as a newborn who just arrived to liberty. Praise God! It was consummated.

EPILOGUE

In the "new world", Gustavo really felt his individual freedom. He went to school and dedicated himself to be a winner. With the help of the Nagy couple, he was able to go to school and learn the Portuguese language. He also earned his degree as an Optician and years later, started his own business. Because his first wife couldn't leave Hungary, through common agreement, they decided to annul the marriage. She in fact got married again a few years later. Gustavo married Aurea, the author of this book, and they had three children: two girls and one boy. In 1988 they moved to the United States of America where they currently reside. In 1990, when the fall of Communism happened in Europe, Gustavo went back to Hungary, but this time in a total different manner: by plane and freely entering the country. After thirty-eight years, he returned to see his native country, family, and friends. It was extremely emotional for him to see his country free of the tyranny of Communism.

This book was written to testify about the atrocities committed in favor of a false and erroneous ideal, and against innocent people. Also, it was written to the glory and praise of God who not only preserved Gustavo's life and his family's, but also allowed him to live in a free country.

I hope this book becomes an incentive to those who have an ideal or a dream to reach, which might seem impossible at the moment, but with courage, persistence, and trust in God, everything is possible.

Aurea Nadasi
Author

****

ABOUT THE COVER

The cover of this book represents Gustavo looking back into his past. The artist, Nicole Campasano, was able to blend in the present and the past by combining a current picture of Gustavo and an old picture of the actual house in which he grew up in Budapest, Hungary.

ISBN 141203002-1

9 781412 030021